CW01646571

ANNEMIEKE HARTMAN JEMMETT

FEAR, TRUST & VALUES

THE POWER OF CHOICE

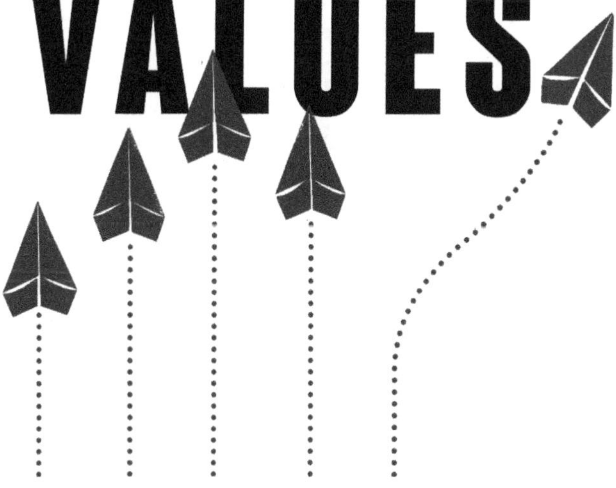

Copyright© 2022 Annemieke Hartman Jemmett

Published by Known Publishing, 2022

The right of Annemieke Hartman Jemmett to be identified as the Author of the Work has been asserted by her in accordance with the Copyright, Designs and Patents Act 1988. All rights reserved.

Paperback: 978-1-913717-87-2

Hardback: 978-1-913717-89-6

Ebook: 978-1-913717-88-9

This book is sold subject to the condition it shall not, by way of trade or otherwise, be circulated in any form or by any means, electronic or otherwise without the publisher's prior consent.

KNOWN

WWW.GET-KNOWN.CO.UK

"Whatever happens in life,
just celebrate it"

- BHAGWAN SHREE RAJNEESH

In Memoriam Jan Anton Hartman

CONTENTS

MY STORIES – THE WILDERNESS...67

MY STORIES – LIFE...89

MY STORIES – WORK...139

STOP FEAR DRIVING YOUR DECISION-MAKING;

TAKE CONTROL, LIVE YOUR VALUES AND BUILD TRUST

No matter where you are in your journey, living life according to your values and building trust will allow you to reach your full potential. If that is too big a statement at this stage, maybe your aim is to enjoy life more, reduce the fear you experience every day and experience true happiness for some (if not all) of the time? This book will offer simple, practical actions to **allow you to take control back**.

Our experiences are all different, yet when reading this book you will come to know that, in essence, they are all the same. We have all been to school, worked in challenging teams, experienced being overwhelmed, and come up against people willing to help and those keen to boycott.

Once you start reading this book, no matter where you start, my story will sound familiar, even though it is not the same as yours. You will find many elements you recognise in your journey; you will become aware, and that is the start to adjusting your response. Each chapter first sets out the challenge we face, while my story sets out the context, and the final element offers practical steps towards taking control – yes, you can!

My promise to you is that, upon completion, you will feel able to more frequently live your values and build trust and, in doing so, you will see the reward: fear will stop driving your decision-making. Once you experience the reward, you will practise and implement living your values more often, taking control more each and every day. Decision-making based on fear will melt away. You will be more in control and, as a result, significantly reduce the risk of burnout.

Let's quickly address that reference to burnout. This book is not focused on preventing burnout. However, being in control allows you to manage during periods of heavy workload and long hours. Living with high fear and uncertainty may make you feel out of control and at risk of burnout. However, being able to see the relationship between fear, trust and values in your everyday life allows you to proactively take back control.

Soon you will find this is a much easier way to live your life, creating the opportunity for you to become the master of your own destiny. Enjoy life – it only happens the once.

THIS BOOK IS FOR

People in work, who want to be more carefree as they live their lives (both private and work) in line with their values, yet find themselves struggling with the fear of loss. This could be losing their job, position in the community, life partner, house or more.

Many of us get caught in the trap that nothing is ever enough – so did I. Pre- and post-pandemic, many of us are struggling with boundaries. Being part of a global workforce or having responsibilities in our communities can start to become very overwhelming. Overlay all this with the digital 'always on' lifestyle, and it is no wonder that burnout and mental challenges are now really impacting many of us.

- Are you fearful of failure?
- Does your job keep you awake at night?
- Have you stopped seeing the big picture?
- Have you experienced a lack of achievement?
- Do you want to take back control and start to enjoy life again?

If you have answered yes to some, many or all of these questions, be comforted in the knowledge that all of us experience some of these feelings and now there is an opportunity to take back control and reduce fear-based actions. I have had exactly the same experiences, and I continue to help and support junior and senior people in the workplace as they take back control. This book will raise your awareness, outline my story to offer you context, and show you that you're not alone. Finally, practical actions you can take right *now* are included in each of the chapters.

THIS BOOK WILL OFFER YOU

My story in an easy-to-read format. It is practical, and you will quickly start to feel its positive impact by following its steps, which will allow you to take back control.

All you need to do is read one chapter. This will offer insight into the challenge my story offers and allow you to take back control, presenting practical actions that are simple to implement and will deliver results for you. In doing so, you will reduce the fear created by decision-making, live to your values and build trust. The added benefit in taking back control is that you reduce the risk of burnout.

Once you have read this book, you will be able to grow in different areas:

FEAR

Fear can be positive. Throughout this book you will become more aware of how to use fear as a positive. Fear keeps you from harm. Once fear is no longer focused on keeping you safe, it is instead driving your decisions to prevent any losses where your life will be negatively impacted. In this book you find insights to help you become aware of how to stop fear taking hold in your everyday life. Once you are aware and able to put the actions into practice, you will start to experience value-based decision-making, through which you can build trust. This instantly and positively enhances your life experiences. It allows you to fully participate in your communities. Remember: fear is a choice.

TRUST

Trust will set you free. Trust is at the heart of everything. You will come to realise, if you do not already, that trust will keep fear at bay. Being able to generate trust builds powerful communities. In a way, trust sets you free! Once you trust that you are able to 'fly', you are able to achieve your objectives and feel fully supported. Upon finishing the book, I challenge you to give yourself permission to take control, live your life to your values and be confident that you have all the answers – because you do. In the way that you approach others, you work on building trust in everything you do. In turn, you will be rewarded by their trust in you, which will set you free.

This book offers you the opportunity to prevent burnout. The assessment you find later in the book will offer insight into how much you are really in control of– or, most likely, how you are at risk of being controlled by– events.

In this book you will hear my story, see that our challenges are very similar and learn tangible actions that will allow you to take back control. By the end of this book you will feel empowered to act and enjoy making a difference to your community.

VALUES

We all have values. From our youth, we start to develop our values. Since then, you may find that you have worked more on the values that are important to you, as you have started to grow up. However, living true to your values in all the situations life throws at you is not always easy.

More and more, businesses are working on their purpose and supporting their values. In the best-case scenario, we would work for a company that is a close match to our values. Let's be honest, though: this is not always possible. In this book you will find practical ways to stay true to your values and actively communicate with others. You will develop the skills you need to take control of what is important to you, offering autonomy and the ability to change behaviours, stop conflict developing, invite broad engagement, improve productivity, have people value your skills and actively participate in seeing the bigger picture.

MEET ANNEMIEKE HARTMAN JEMMETT

Hornindal Rundt, the ultramarathon that takes place in early July in Norway, is possibly the best way to describe me. Not the event itself, but some of the key observations that are related to it: the lead up, the event and the follow-up.

As a Dutch national, and most recently a post-Brexit dual national, I was almost 'born on a bike'. An active lifestyle is in our blood, and it starts with mastering the art of cycling; cycling for fun progresses to cycling to school and then cycling long distances to offer getting fit and thinking time– at least, it did for me. When asked by a work colleague to participate in this ultramarathon event, I had to think. His comment was still ringing in my ears: 'I asked you because you are always up for something and I need somebody to join me on this challenge.'

Used to jumping in with both feet, presenting myself with too much of a challenge too quickly, I decided to ask for a seven-day consideration window. Was I really going to be able to do this? Running was not really my thing. The event was a year away; did I really want to dedicate a year to supporting somebody else's challenge? I was flattered to be asked; it showed that I had no ego and that I was keen to support others. Could I turn this also into my challenge? Without too much research or additional considerations, in line with the motto 'jump and the net will appear', I managed to fully commit within the seven-day time frame. 'Let's do it.'

I started training to be in the best shape possible to enjoy the gruelling challenge. Some might ask, 'What is an ultramarathon?' It is anything longer than a marathon (26 miles and 385 yards or 42.195km). However, this was that one stage more challenging. Did you know Norway had mountains? Yes, mountains!

I came to the start line well prepared. I had told everybody about signing up, so I had to do it; failure was not an option. But OMG, this was not running – this was fell running. And yes, I can tell you there is a difference! A big difference. The next 14 hours were an onslaught on my body and soul. Sheer determination was what got us there, and even though we finished last, we made it! Yes, that is no exaggeration; over the previous hours, we had managed to run over the snow line (in *July*!), hang off mountainous hills (lose your grip and you are gone… I was well insured and had taken out a special extreme sports insurance) and unintentionally do the splits in the middle of a field while not breaking anything. Go me! We were exhausted throughout, and I experienced real primal fear. On occasion, that fear kept me safe, but at other times during the 'run'… Well, it almost completely paralysed me. The mantras 'this too will pass' and 'just keep going forward' were ringing in my ears throughout. I will save you the finer details of wading through the waterfalls, being completely soaked throughout part of it and more– much more. During this 'ordeal' (which was fun, challenging and frustrating in equal measure) I knew one thing: no matter what, my running partner and I had each other's back for the total run. We knew we could trust each other.

Why do I tell you this as an overview of 'who wrote this book?' Well, this is to share with you that I have lived and had amazing experiences and continue to do so. Although my running days are firmly over, I am keen to share my experiences as a lot of learning came from this time – and by going on this book journey with me, you will be able to reflect on yours. You can take your learning and reflect on how you can gain control and choose your path in life.

The above story highlights my **relationship with fear**; sometimes it is there to keep you safe, other times it can be completely debilitating for you or the team or people around you. You have to watch out for that.

Values are there from the day you are born but, as you develop, you may refocus them. In this story, you will see that the values of supporting others, authenticity, being inquisitive, keeping things simple and, most of all, enjoying yourself (although it may not sound like it, there was enjoyment in the day) did stand me in good stead in the lead up, during the event and after it. Although I have to admit that I have not participated in a run since!

Critically important throughout was the fact that we knew we could trust each other. We did not live close enough to train together, but we both knew that we would put in the effort, so we could not let each other down. We arranged to meet at the event and turned up on time. We stuck together throughout to make sure that we supported each other. We celebrated the highs and were there to work through the hard times together too. When we fell, we checked each other out and pushed on. When the fear of heights became too overwhelming, we coached each other to keep going forward. The trust on that day was unbreakable.

CONNECT WITH ME ON SOCIAL MEDIA

annemieke.hartmanjemmett

timezonepix

HOW TO USE THIS BOOK

This book provides the opportunity for you to take back control. Of what, that is for you to decide. Fear, trust and values are in direct relation to each other. It is a continuous sliding scale; the key is to tip the balance of the scale towards values for as much as possible, in turn maximising the building of trust.

MINDSET

My aim with this book is for you to become more aware of some simple actions that put you in control of your life. You will get the best experience if you are 'brave' in your daily life and implement some or all of the actions set out in the 'Take control' sections of the book. You will be rewarded, but to what extent is down to you. Be confident and trust in your own ability; you have it in you to live your life according to your values and build trust within your community. Maybe this book is the first step of many towards you achieving your full potential.

BEFORE YOU READ ANY FURTHER

I have worked as a coach with many people and teams. Key to their success is providing a benchmark, allowing them to assess how far they have come after investing some of their time. You are amazing, and this benchmark is going to show you exactly how you have progressed after investing some time in reading my story and completing some (or all) of the tasks presented.

It is important to point out that you do not have to do it all at once. However, I predict that as soon as you start to experience the rewards, you will want to do more and more.

I recommend that you take this assessment before starting the book and do it again at the end. It gives you a clear indicator of how you have made progress in allowing yourself to take back control.

How to complete this assessment: read each bullet and score how you assess your feelings. Give yourself permission to share how you really feel in the answers. You do not have to share this with anyone, so you can be fair to yourself. You are reading this book to take back control, so you should give yourself every opportunity to do so.

INITIAL ASSESSMENT

I have the ability to change behaviour in others.	Agree/Unsure/ Disagree
I lack control.	Agree/Unsure/ Disagree
I dislike work.	Agree/Unsure/ Disagree
I lack the skills to do my job.	Agree/Unsure/ Disagree
I don't see the big picture.	Agree/Unsure/ Disagree
I am not really able to engage.	Agree/Unsure/ Disagree
I maximise my productivity whenever I can.	Agree/Unsure/ Disagree
Tasks I have to do seem to take a lot of effort.	Agree/Unsure/ Disagree
I believe challenging conversations are a form of conflict.	Agree/Unsure/ Disagree
I am stuck.	Agree/Unsure/ Disagree

RESOURCE PACK

The resource pack is there for you! It provides the following FREE tools to start supporting your journey towards taking control and living the life that you choose:

- A downloadable workbook, including the assessment for you to complete at the start and again upon completion of the book; this offers you control and tracks your results.
- The opportunity to book a FREE 20-minute call with me to chat through your journey; I am interested to learn more.
- A postcard to write down your fears on and an address to post it to, anonymously.
- Access to the Fear, Trust and Values Community: a community of people who are proactive in managing fear, choose to behave according to their values and build trust; sharing allows us to grow.
- An explanation of the three-dimensional communication diagram.
- Access to other multi-media, including videos and articles.
- Opportunities for collaborations.

You can access the Resource Pack here:

www.annemiekehartmanjemmett.com

FUTURE PACE

Well done for taking the first step towards exploring further, being open to diverse inputs and challenging yourself. You are wanting to make the choices that are the right ones for you, acting from the perspective of your values and not from a place of fear. It can be good for you to be 'nosey', because other people's stories and experiences are interesting. My story is just that – mine. As you will see, my life has not always been easy, even though many have thought (and told me) that it was all straightforward for me.

I am sharing my story so that any learning that may have taken me years to develop can be offered to you in an easy-to-understand way and is simple to implement.

I wrote this book to show you that you can live the life you choose.

You want a life where you live to your values and continuously build trust in personal and work situations. Fear will become something you can embrace, using it to keep yourself safe, and so have a healthy relationship with it. You will be rewarded by engaging in more opportunities, with people presenting themselves to help and support. You will start to develop around you a like-minded community. In doing so, you will also start to notice that others around you will be more open to you and share their experiences and challenges, offering you the opportunity to support them. In doing so, you are collectively choosing to live according to your values, building trust and creating a community that is worthwhile. For personal situations, it means you can engage in the things that are of real interest to you, and you will be appreciated and rewarded in equal measure. For businesses, you will find that you have high engagement from individuals, resulting in great team cohesion and a true living of the values. In all cases, trust will continue to strengthen and grow.

FOREWORD

There is value in values; linking fear to values and bringing in the dynamic of trust proves to be a complex topic. In the end, you come to realise that fear, trust and values move seamlessly along a linear slider and the smoother we can make it, with the bulk of the team weight on the side of trust and values, the more personal satisfaction and contentment we can achieve.

Many have asked me to explain who this book is for or my reason for writing it – or both and more! This is the book I wish I had been able to read before I started off in my life. Yes, life – not just work life, but also personal life. This book is all about creating awareness of how fear, trust and values are all directly related to each other and how the pendulum swings continuously between all three. In fully understanding their relationship to each other, we are able to significantly reduce the risk of burnout.

I want to start a conversation that is more dynamic, taking into consideration that we have members in our teams who are fearful, and we have a responsibility to support them through effective communication. In all cases we *must*, as leaders, ask ourselves the same question: are we leading from a fear position? If so, we must be brave and take appropriate action. I do live in the real world, however, and see fear driving actions far too often.

This book provides insight into the way that I see the world, my perspective. Therefore, it is not intended to be a single source of 'the truth', but another personal story that is shared authentically. Throughout, I provide insight, personality, experiences, lots of analogies to offer detail and, overall, a pragmatic and simple outline that you – if it's appropriate and relevant – can try out to improve your success, not only at work but in life, and reduce fear-based behaviour across the team (yes, that may include you). Because that is exactly what matters: your life!

If you are looking for a book that is solely based on fact and fully evidenced data, presented with extensive references, stop reading – this book is not for you! There are many books that take care of that requirement– just not this one.

Those of you who are interested in the experiences of a bilingual commercial expert, professional, world traveller and global citizen, with over 35 years' experience in high-pressured global roles delivering unbelievable results – without suffering burnout (but getting close at times, I realise now) – based on a sound education, both practical as well as academic, being pragmatic and extremely impatient, then read on!

Everything I do is based on my unwavering belief that I can achieve *anything*. Well, maybe not truly anything, but definitely everything that sits within my sphere of control. You will start to find out more of this detail as you work your way through the book.

I live by a set number of values. They are that:

- I must be **authentic** in everything I do.
- I strive to be **inquisitive** and ask lots of questions; we do so when we are children, so why do we lose this ability when we grow up?
- Everything needs to be **simple** because only then will we be able to actually action things and get engagement.
- **Creativity** drives life and stops it being boring; it is also the real secret to my success.
- **Pleasure** is important. In case you had not yet noticed, life has a finite end – we just don't know when that may be. This means that during our lives we may as well have and create pleasure every day.

There will be more on my values throughout. This is the essence of what I will be exploring and it should give you a good idea and help you decide whether this book is for you. You may find some well-researched data inside it – great!– but you will find mainly experiences, outcomes, insights, recommendations and explorations based on common sense (and my personal well-balanced perspective). These will be very easy to use and implement with great success for you.

Intrigued? Great, then join me on the journey!

INTRODUCTION

Here we go! I procrastinated for nine months before I had the courage to sit down and write this book about fear, trust and values. Having spent 38.5 years (yes, that's the exact figure for 2022) in work life, I believe I have a story to tell that may resonate with many of you.

This insight is about my experience throughout these years, all seen through my lens. You can never start to tell the story just based on work life. You have to start from the real beginning: how you came into this world, what happened in those formative years. All those seemingly mundane events have shaped me into what I am today. The first 17.5 years created the base from which everything flows.

Throughout my life I have been interested in reading other people's stories, in particular those who have 'made it big', preferably through adversity. To sit down now and write mine seems a bit unreal and a true luxury – but hey, why not? 'It had better be good,' I hear you say; well, we will just have to see. Life is a journey full of twists and turns. Each personal story is unique, and does it really matter if you have 'made it big'? What does 'big' mean? And by whose measure? Each personal story is worthwhile and an opportunity to reflect, absorb and sometimes even learn.

In my life I have been fortunate enough to meet many different people from many different cultures, and to travel extensively for work. Throughout, I have become aware that I am 'different' – I will aim to cover how in each part of this book. Everybody is interested in 'secrets' and, if mine can be nicely packaged in an easy-to-understand storyline, who would possibly want to hold you back?

So why 'fear, trust and values'? As you will come to read, we all are brought up with a set of values. Yet when you are 'let loose' in the open world and have to start to fend for yourself, something else creeps in, called Fear. Fear can be good, as it will make you stop and think (a kind of safety mechanism) when looking around; however, fear is now often the driver to stop – or worse, suspend – your decision-making to cover your own backside in your career. If the decision cannot be pinned on you, the status quo continues and life is good. But is it really? This is for you to decide each and every day.

Yesterday I went for lunch with a business connection who has really, throughout the years, become a friend. He asked a sound question. 'Annemieke, who are you writing the book for?'

In reality, this book is for a number of people:

- Young people who are keen to learn and hear different stories.
- Professionals who are frustrated at being negatively impacted by others who work in a fear-driven way

rather than looking to identify behaviours that support their values (both personal and business).

- Business executives and leaders who know they can make a difference but are looking for more guidance on how to change organisations and improve team member engagement.
- Others who have 'brushed past' me in life and are interested in understanding more about me.

You can call this book an addition to my CV, if you like. Recently I was told I get things done, and I think that is a pretty good summary.

With this intro, buckle up and enjoy the ride!

PERSONAL BELIEFS

In this book, I have focused on staying balanced throughout. I work from the belief that everybody, from the outset, has the intention to be supportive of each other. In general, and in essence, people are in a job to provide for the people they hold dear. Many of us, however, lose perspective along the way, but this is not intentional; deep-rooted beliefs are at the core of this development.

Throughout this book, you will see me sharing my experiences in corporate and private life. This is not to shame people who have worked with me (don't worry: no company or people names are included!), but I have a variety of experiences that I will share with you. I believe the other people involved acted with the best intentions, but they were sometimes just ill-informed, poorly educated or did not think about their impact on others – time had not taught them the lessons they still had to learn. We all are somewhere on that line of development.

The stories I walk you through are included merely to illustrate the message I would like to deliver in each section. The purpose of sharing the stories is to bring to life the challenges and the need to take control, and for you the reader to be able to reflect on them and take simple actions that are going to offer you that control. No doubt you all have your own very interesting stories to tell, and they would fit nicely within the chapters of this book that you are about to read. If you cannot wait to share your fear, trust and/or values, there are opportunities to do so at the end of the book.

This book can be read from the start or from back to front. Or, if you prefer, you could start somewhere in the middle; that is also OK. Take from it what is of value to you; review it, hold it against the light and apply it in a way that works for you. It would be valuable to improve interaction and communication between individuals and teams based on the development of shared values and, if they are not shared, for whatever reason, make sure they are understood from individual to individual and across the teams; this will help with the creation of respect, a key foundation.

If we are all able to achieve this common understanding or sharing of values, fear will reduce at the same time. Although fear will protect us in a primal way, in most normal situations fear can prevent us from achieving the maximum result; it is like having team members who constantly drive with the brakes on. It's a great way of staying in control, but it wears the system out much faster than if you just let go. If you have four different team members managing one wheel each, and they have the ability to brake autonomously, it starts to get dangerous; the wrong combination of speed and braking quickly sends the car out of control, with the distinct possibility that it will flip over, with disastrous results. It is all about setting joint goals while braking at the same time to keep control. Communication, finding alignment and, at the core, treating each other with respect will get results for all.

See, there you go – that's the first analogy, and it is still only the introduction.

Still, you should always remember that with belief you can truly achieve *anything*.

MY PERSPECTIVE – THE REFERENCE BACKGROUND

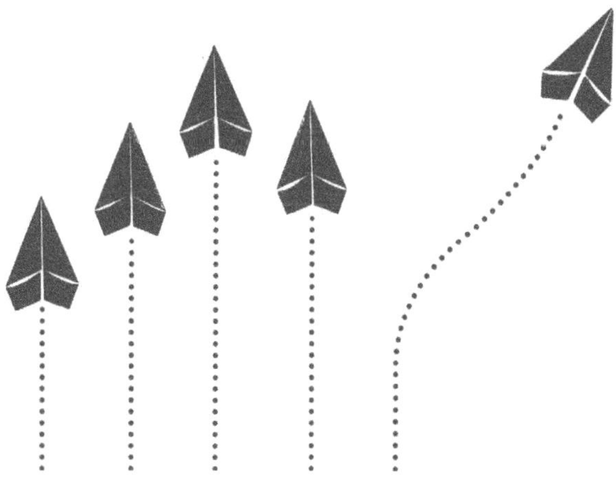

Now that we are all fully connected 24/7, we have different ways to 'work through information' compared with earlier generations. There is 'always-on' access to websites, social media, information channels, news (plus fake news), virtual and face-to-face communities, friends and more– much more. Many people are finding it difficult to keep up with this constant stream of information. Demands on your time and inputs are out of control, if you let them drive you.

On top of the indirect information channels, we also have a requirement to respond to emails (both private and business), WhatsApp and direct SMS (text) messages and those (now quite old-fashioned) phone calls.

Instagram, Facebook and LinkedIn require posts and innovative comments just to show that you are 'on the ball' and engaging.

Gosh, just writing this makes me realise again that we need to be so careful not to get 'sucked in' to becoming 'busy fools'. With all of the above you find that others set your agenda for the day. If you are unfortunate and unclear on your values or struggle to stick to them because they are at odds with the company or community values, then you are at great risk of things coming off the rails. If not kept in check, you may run the risk of burnout.

Why is there such a clear requirement to have and give instant responses? Is it really acceptable for our networks to expect us to be on 24/7? Yes! Unless we change the pace for ourselves. Easier said than done, I hear you say, and I totally agree. However, once you start to take your first tentative steps and to gain results from this book and the accompanying workbook, I can guarantee you will do more of it.

A simple and practical tip to prevent burnout, although it is challenging, is to take control. Start by 'contracting' to the people you are in contact with. Create boundaries by setting expectations, make sure you talk them through and get agreement. It is easier to discuss this rather than trying to achieve it through SMS or WhatsApp; the discussion is delicate, and we must ensure that we listen as well as talk– receive as well as send. Most importantly, whatever you agree, stick to it: deliver on your promise. This means if you say you will respond within 24 hours – do it! If you agree not to respond after 18:00, stick to it – *don't* respond after 18:00.

An additional action that is simple to implement is to plan your day through your diary. This is how to do it:

- Structurally create 'breathing spaces' in your day– one lunch break of 45 minutes, and two 20-minute breaks, one in the morning and one in the afternoon.
- Book meetings for less than 60 minutes– 45 minutes' 'talk time' with a 15-minute wrap-up post meeting.
- Insert project times in your diary– this is where you work on projects.

- Batch your emails during work, at the beginning, middle and end of the day – 20 minutes each.
- Block one hour each day to work through emails that require you to provide more detail or complete a request at short notice.
- Negotiate project delivery times. It may be urgent for others, so share your availability and support where possible, but you do need to keep it within your availability.
- Provide insight into your diary.
- Block your diary until you start and block your diary after you finish.
- Be flexible throughout in line with the needs of the business.

Planning your diary will allow you more control over your time, and it will get you to focus during the day. You will be amazed to see what you can achieve. This starts to work well on offering you control, gives you choice and autonomy, and adds value to all.

This is because, when we look closely – yes, come forward a bit more... get even closer – **it is all down to our own behaviour, our values and our boundaries.**

PURPOSE

As you progress through life and achieve things you would never have thought possible, you start to ask yourself different questions. I decided to talk to a coaching professional, engaging in a year-long programme to create a framework to guide me towards finding answers to the question: 'I am living my best life today but am I prepared to also live my best life tomorrow?' This allowed me to hold the values that guided me for the last 50 years up against the light. More interestingly, I found that some of the values just did not work in the format in which I had developed them so many years ago. Here is a value that effectively outlines why I needed to do this:

Since I was young, I have been living with one of my values being honesty. Now we would probably all say that honesty is a great value and no doubt many parents explain to their children that honesty is key in life. I don't disagree with that position, but in life I started to get stuck with honesty as a key value. Of course, it is helpful to be **honest** throughout your life. However, there are periods in your life when you are confronted with situations where being completely honest is just not wholly possible.

HONEST
/'änəst/

ADJECTIVE:
Sincere and free of deceit

SIMILAR:
truthful, sincere, candid, frank, direct, open, forthright, straight, straightforward, genuine, blunt, plain-spoken, outspoken, upfront, objective, impartial, unbiased, balanced, unprejudiced, disinterested, even-handed, fair, just, equitable

OPPOSITE:
insincere, biased

In other words, **the dictionary definition of honesty is: always telling the truth, and never stealing or cheating**.

In reviewing the exact details, I can totally see that I apply a lot of honesty to my day-to-day communications – those of you who know me would certainly be able to recognise me in these words of clarification that you have just read above. However, there are times when it just does not totally cover everything.

As an example, the company I worked for was hitting some stormy weather financially, and doing business was challenging. Somehow, the company had not previously come up against this; it had created a significantly high cost base from its inception, to date unnoticed, and was already overstretched. Its very costly production platform, linked to an extreme abundance of employees, was untenable (there was a whole bunch of other stuff going on, but I will spare you the detail). Then the Covid-19 pandemic kicked in and there was no further room for error – things had to change. I was one of the first ones calling for change – quick action to steady the ship.

We needed the best of the best to stand a good chance of steadying the ship. Several months later, a redundancy process was started. I fought for the high performers in the team – as they would be the ones who would be able to deliver the company's budgeted success. The outcome, however, was more based on 'old beliefs', seeing some non-performing team members as 'talismans' and making decisions based on people they liked rather than their ability to perform to the set goals. This meant that I was aware of the challenges very early on in the process. I also knew the end result – who would be asked to leave and who would be able to stay – if not overtly, then definitely instinctively. Was this the time to be honest? Yes, within the decision-making team, but no in terms of the team members who were going to be affected. I had a duty to the company, and timing at that point was everything. So my 'honesty' to the team members was to say they were at risk, although I was not yet able to share who would stay and who would go.

So the detail behind what honesty means is key here; timing is everything, as there are serious legal implications if you share information ahead of the formal communication. Clearly, this had not been the first time in my life when I was presented with this kind of situation. Previously, it did not sit well with me either, but it had never motivated me to think about the issue differently or, better still, get me to challenge my own beliefs. The life coaching that I started worked on my own purpose and beliefs, with supporting values to bring all this work together.

My experience throughout this process was that I could define my beliefs much more easily than my purpose. In this example, I can highlight that I swapped honesty out for *authenticity*. People around me understand that I hold a position of authority, keeping their best interests at the core of what I do, but that I also have a responsibility to the company to act in its best interest (incidentally, they are also the ones who pay me). You can see this is an impossible position, if you are guided by honesty only. For this reason, I have changed this for me to authenticity. I am true to my beliefs and will act in an honest way. The people who know me would say I am always a good communicator: open, clear and fair in my approach. During these processes I can say that I am not at liberty to share information at a certain stage. This, for me, is truer to my newly assigned value than the 'old' value of honesty.

There will be many instances in this book where you are able to see the values in action.

As a reminder, here are my values:

- I must be **authentic** in everything I do.
- I strive to be **inquisitive** and ask lots of questions.
- Everything needs to be **simple**.
- **Creativity** drives life and stops it being boring; it is also the real secret to my success.
- **Pleasure** is important, because life has a finite end.

MY PURPOSE

How do you define your purpose? This is much, much harder than defining your values. This has taken me a full year of hard work to define, and I am still not sure that it won't change in the years to come.

Finally, I managed to establish my purpose after a lot of reading.

Before I share my purpose, I came across an update to my coach. I wrote:

'This is the big question for me. To try to solve it, I have decided to engage one of my values – being inquisitive – so I have started to ask other people what they believe their purpose is. The answers are really fascinating.

I have had a mix of responses, some very business-like (all Dutch people take that approach) and very simple. Other people's purpose responses were:

- Based on reincarnation, constantly learning with an aim to share and grow (new neighbour), and he practises it well.
- Simplifying their lives for happiness.
- Letting their kids flourish and be grounded.

My first attempt, for my own clarity, offered up the following words – I hasten to add there is more work I want to do on this question:

- Broaden my horizons.
- Have cultural interests.
- Have strategic commercial insights.
- Consider different perspectives – share these in discussion.
- Allow others to take this information and use it for their own gain (intellectual, spatial, commercial or otherwise).

Other words that I have listed for Purpose are:

- Personal growth
- Exploring
- Developing
- Growth
- Learning
- Awareness
- Work in progress.

PURPOSE 2022

As you can see, a lot of work has gone in to defining the purpose. For now, I have settled on a forward motion purpose:

Explore; Create; Grow.

INSIGHT: FEAR AND VALUES

FEAR

Once you start to research fear, you come to all kinds of conclusions. My first one was that fear does not have to be bad! That was an eye opener for me. Fear keeps you from harm, which is good. Humans are told to fear the unknown. Fear also stops you doing things, which in some situations might be good. In case you decide that it is good to jump off a four-storey building without precautions, you really want fear to kick in, because jumping will hurt and may jeopardise your life.

It may not be so good, though, if it stops you going out of the house to do your shopping for fear of being run over! Anyhow, you get the gist. Fear is helpful and you should take it into consideration, but you should not let it define you. The details, of course, will be different for each and every one of us.

Directly linked to fear is risk-taking. This is different for each and every one of us, too. I am, for instance, a *big* risk taker. Not quite the person who jumps from a high building without preparation and expects everything to be alright– but with great preparation, you can get really high up the building and jump off safely.

Now comes the question: is a big risk really that bad? In my opinion, all day we make decisions to engage or not to engage; to sit back and let it all happen to us or to be the one that leads and guides. I can, hand on heart, say that I am definitely the one who leads and guides (anybody who knows me will agree) and therefore I am often frustrated by the pace and level of engagement of other people. So I take a lot of time planning and looking at my next steps in great detail, but quickly; and based upon my experience, I can assess outcomes based on actions in a dynamic model.

In my view the risks I take are well considered, reviewed and therefore calculated with a good chance of the desired successful outcome. That is how I deliver great results, while to others the decisions I make might seem like big risks that are not worth taking. More about that later.

I have worked extensively with groups of commercial experts (and not so expert) on understanding the decision-making process in a commercial setting. The conversation goes something like this. You are presenting to the decision-maker and have managed to do everything right: you have shown them the detail, outlined the return on investment, etc. etc. Now it is down to the decision-maker to make the choice: yes or no? Award the contract or keep looking? This is where commercial engagement can start to drift, sometimes for really long periods of time, resulting in the imminent danger of losing the opportunity.

The most important question the commercial expert (and not so expert) can ask now will focus on really understanding the fears that are driving the decision-maker. Yes, this is a real thing! They will be influenced by events that are totally not apparent to you.

Some examples are:

- In one of their previous roles, the decision-maker made the wrong decision, and it cost the company significant revenue opportunities. Nobody has found out, but the decision-maker knows! They have managed to cover it up effectively, so no damage has been done to them personally, yet this event impacts them every day of their working life. In this case, you need to give assurances that you are the lowest-risk option in securing the deal.

- The decision-maker grew up in a really poor family background that has impacted their life and still affects their decision-making every day; they do not want to go back there. The decision-maker does *everything* to make sure they decide based on their own best outcome, and from time to time this will coincide with the best solution for the business. More frequently than you imagine, this will be the best outcome for the decision-maker.

Reflecting on the above, I have to add the most critical action you can take:

- Stop using the one-dimensional communication model – this means stop telling people what you have got to offer. The chance that you will hit the jackpot in communicating what they need, I guess, is 10%, unless you are absolutely unique in your offering (and if this is the case, you may as well sell online with the lowest possible cost base and no interaction). Instead, use the three-dimensional communication model. Listen to your customers. *Ask* them what they would fear most, and let them tell you what they *need*. Understand who in the world is offering the same or similar cheaper– in other words, who your competitors are– and then pitch. I can guarantee your success rate will go up exponentially, because in doing so you have created the most important element of communication: trust! By understanding what your customer fears most, you can address this head on.

VALUES

In the introduction I shared my values with you. They provide clear guidance to me; call it my internal compass. Now, to live by these each and every day is not always as easy as it looks. Daily, there is a constant balancing between survival, compromise and much more. What I have learned is to align my values with those of the communities I engage in. I have enough examples that show me that, if I do not do this, I will end up in conflict (mostly with myself) and there is a danger I may quickly compromise my own wellbeing.

During the writing of this book, and in the many years leading up to it, I have been discussing values with the smallest and biggest business owners and executives and have only come to one conclusion. Values are specific to each business; they are individual and will only be impactful if they are genuine and developed through team engagement. They may have been developed at a moment in time, yet they offer a living and breathing core for the business, so creating relevant context each and every day makes it possible for individuals and teams to own them.

Values are not just words that look good in marketing materials; they need to have content and context and to be driven by purpose. If they do this, they will enhance your materials and become the cornerstone of your communications. In turn, this will build trust and drive real engagement for commercial gain, keeping fear at bay.

Thanks to all of you who have helped me come to this insight.

INNATE VS LEARNED

In several conversations I had when researching this book, we touched on the words 'fear' and 'values' and had extensive discussions on whether these are innate or learned. This piqued my interest some more, so I decided to start at the beginning and look both terms up in the dictionary for some more background.

Being bilingual, speaking both Dutch and English, I find great value in fully understanding the meaning rather than assuming that I know what it really means. For your reference, I have included the dictionary findings. When you read through this detail, it helps with the clarification of the detail on fears and values that I discussed above.

A shorthand overview outline would be that fear is a primal part of 'you', while values are quite the opposite: you have made them your own from a very early age, and they are learned. What I have come to find out for myself is that my values were those that I had created when I was young. In my early fifties, through the events that I describe in this book, I decided to question them; I held them up against the light while engaging in a year's worth of 'life coaching'. I cannot say that they completely changed – but I can confirm that they are now enhanced and have become personal values that I feel are innate – they are totally natural to me, and I live my life with them at its core.

Moral understanding is not the only thing that changes as people mature; people's values tend to change over time, as well. Humanist psychologists propose that people have an **innate** sense of values and personal preferences that tends to get buried under layers of social demands and expectations (social mores).

When researching innate versus learned values, the conversation can be infinite. The discussion here is only meant to be a reference for scene setting, not a comprehensive overview.

INNATE

/ɪ'neɪt,'ɪneɪt/

ADJECTIVE:

Something that comes naturally

SIMILAR:

inborn, natural, congenital, inherent, intrinsic, instinctive, intuitive, unlearned, untaught, hereditary, inherited, in the blood, quintessential, organic, essential, fundamental, built-in, inbuilt, ingrown, deep-rooted, connate, connatural

OPPOSITE:

acquired

Now that you have further insight into fear and its origins for you, we can 'hoover up' and explore the difference between fear and values. Fear is something that is in you. The above overview provided in the dictionary offers a good insight into its meaning.

This does not, however, mean that you cannot control it, but there is a need to recognise its origins.

Once you are clear of your position in relation to fear, then you can hold it against the light and put it into context for you in relation to values.

LEARN

/ləːn/

VERB:

To gain knowledge of or acquire a skill in something by experience, study or being taught

SIMILAR:

acquire a knowledge of, gain an understanding of, become competent in, become proficient in, grasp, master, take in, absorb, pick up, digest, become expert in, know inside out, know backwards, comprehend, study, work at, apply oneself to, be taught, pursue, get the hang of, get clued up about, commit to memory

OPPOSITE:

forget

TRUST

When I started writing this book, 'trust' did not feature in the title; the book was going to be called *Fear and Values*. Yet it soon became blatantly obvious that everything about the way we operate comes from trust, both in personal as well as business life.

If we take a look at advertising and look beyond the veneer, it is all about the creation of trust and, as per the wise words of Mac Cato (of the agency Wunderman Cato Johnson), one of my mentors, 'brands are in the business of creating longing and belonging'.

Trust is set in the middle of the title on purpose. Fear, trust and values form a continuous linear movement, a sliding scale if you will, and are ever present. The key is taking control. Fundamental to reducing fear and maximising values-based behaviour is engaged communication.

Leaders who are prepared to put listening (receiving) at the heart of everything they do will find that they create the maximum amount of trust while finding excellent engagement from their teams.

In most cases, leaders find this difficult, as it is 'easier' to take control (is that not what you are supposed to do?) and lead the way. But if we look at leaders who maximised the engagement of their teams, they are the most successful. They show that the saying 'many hands make light work' does apply to them.

Leaders who have a misplaced sense of responsibility, the 'doing it all yourself' types, lack engagement and participation, resulting in reduced results and, in short, an uphill struggle. The uphill struggle can manifest itself in exhaustion, frustration, burnout or other health-related issues.

Once we understand that trust is at the heart of everything we do, then (and only then) we know how we need to adjust our behaviour to reduce fear and maximise trust through the development and implementation of values.

MY STORIES – THE WILDERNESS

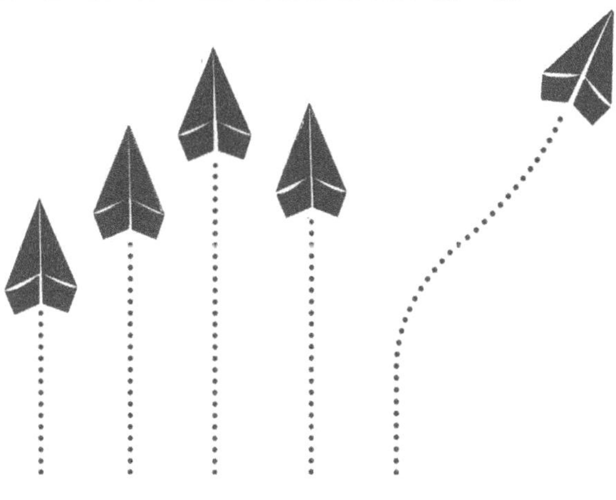

MISTAKES OF A LIFETIME

CHALLENGE

Ups and downs, and still standing.

MY STORY

In reading this book, you may start to think that my life was without any hiccups. Those of you who have lived to a more mature age know that this, of course, never happens. Life is a series of ups and downs, and you live with the hope that the ups are more frequent than the downs. Or, if this is not the case, that you can get enough energy from the ups for you to be able to ride out the downs.

I have indeed been fortunate. I was born into a family that was very balanced and caring, with a great focus on education, development and personal exploration. Having not been baptised, I was told that my religion going forward was completely my choice. To date, I would still say that I am 'without religion'. However, I have read up on all sorts of religions and convictions, including Catholicism, Protestantism, Buddhism, Scientology and other creeds. None of them have convinced me to join their beliefs in such a way that I am completely dedicated to them. What I do adhere to, and try to live by each day, is the idea that we should be kind to others.

Anyhow, I digress. In life we make many mistakes each day, and from these mistakes we learn. They are very varied for me. Once I returned from a long travelling trip in the evening and, not wanting to miss out on some fun, I joined friends to go to an event. There I mis-stepped and managed to break my jaw in three places (I can recommend this for quick weight loss). At another point, I also opted to work in the UK without having my accommodation prearranged, meaning I ended up somewhere weird and wonderful.

From a business perspective, I started a pet business. The concept was tried and tested– we were going to offer services covered by insurance– but we needed three locations to make this work. The most important thing I learned was that, if you want to be successful here, you need a lot of money to get things off the ground. It did get off the ground but the investments in the longer term were not sustainable out of my own funds. I also pitched the concept to the UK's largest pet store and, even though they were not interested, they did start this kind of business a few years later. Coincidence? Maybe.

Another initiative was the invention of a way to measure noise in the workplace. The maximum legal limit was set at 80 dB, and a simple hand-held tool offered an opportunity to measure the levels. It was a great invention and we sold many. A few years later this became possible on a mobile, but we were too late to develop the app. So it was a flash-in-the-pan success and soon obsolete. All these mistakes would probably be really good content for another book!

In reading the events above, you can see that engagement without debilitating fear (remember that a healthy amount of fear is good), and fully based on values, offers a great chance for success, but success is not guaranteed. If you are able to trust in your own ability, you can achieve great things – if you are prepared to learn from experience.

Don't assume from the little information I have provided here that I have not been through the wringer. There have been times where I could have lost it all. This possibly tells you that I am ready to take risks, but the mere fact that I have not lost it all yet shows that the risks are well considered. Even if things go off track, I now know that I am able to be creative in ensuring they come back in line.

Have I learned from my mistakes? Absolutely. Do they make me who I am? Absolutely. Will I make more mistakes? Absolutely. Do they define me? Absolutely not.

Finding time to reflect on my mistakes, having taken the time to re-evaluate my values in a year-long process, is now setting me up to accept change each and every day; and not only to accept change but to actively anticipate and work with it. Change is inevitable, so getting rid of fear within this setting has, for me, been critical to the enjoyment of life. If you suffer from debilitating fear, then all you are doing is impacting your own life each and every day. And really, what is the worst that can happen?

THE WORST THAT CAN HAPPEN

After making many mistakes in life, what is the worst that can happen (we are excluding physical harm here)? You lose it all. If you lose it all but you have been kind to others, I find that others are kind to you in return. By being authentic, inquisitive and creative, by keeping things simple and having pleasure in what you do, you will always be able to find kindness, a place to live and a place to 'work'. You will do something for which you will get paid.

To date, this has worked out OK. Let's see what happens next.

TAKE CONTROL

- **Fear:** Keep it in check, because fear is a choice. Make sure it is not debilitating.

- **Trust:** It will come right; you are exactly where you need to be.

- **Values:** If you have been kind to others, you will find you will get kindness back in spades. It is exactly the same with other values. Put out there what you want to see back.

STORIES FROM THE WILDERNESS

Every company will be keen these days to make its values known to employees and customers alike. This is not new, of course. In the 1980s, one of my first senior jobs working for a global company started with the receipt of a credit card-sized piece of branded card outlining the company's key values. The supporting message was to learn the values off by heart! The intention was clearly coming from a genuine and, at its core, a good place – but the application was flawed from the outset.

Here it is also good to highlight that fear is directly linked to the 'bad' implementation of values. You may feel this already without me having to explain it. If the values are clear and communicated comprehensively and, if possible, are specific to both the company and the individual, this will bring great security. You can also call it the creation of trust– and, if you trust, you can achieve anything.

Now, in life we almost get brought up to distrust; at every twist and turn we ask ourselves the question, 'Is this what I expected?' We follow that with, 'Are they telling the truth? Is this too good to be true?' With scams on the increase, we train ourselves to consistently ask these qualifying questions. This is good to keep us safe. What does it do, however, to the relationship between our fears and our values? If the values are not genuine, we will question why, and if we do so and we start to become insecure, fear sets in and quickly takes over.

Throughout my career, I have come across many good and well-intended ideas in this space. However, when you hold the application to the light, it becomes clear that there is still a lot of work to do. I have not shared the identity of the individuals or companies as it adds nothing to the points I would like to highlight, but I know who they are, and for those who read the book, they may recognise the events and situations. Many would no doubt like to forget they even happened.

VALUES WITH CONVICTION

For a few years, I worked for a global manufacturing company. One of the reasons for joining them was their strong culture across the company. They were excellent and strong at communicating this in their collateral: brochures, websites and other communications. When it came to personal communications, however, they were downright weak. Initially, I thought this was quite funny, but the longer I was involved, the more embarrassing it became.

When employees were presenting, the conversation inevitably came to the values and how these were driving the company forward; they majored in highlighting how different the company was in the industry, and they could really pull off the motivational 'speech'. However, when it came down to the individual values – there were five – they could consistently produce only four of the five values in the summing up. Not only was it embarrassing, but it was an immediate attack on the trust position they had tried to create, a bit like an own goal.

Having experienced this disaster more than once, the company decided to rebrand itself. And with this process came a new set of values that were easy to remember and explain, although they were not that different from the original ones, being genuine and at the core of the business. I attended our first exhibition, and our CEO had decided that the values needed an acronym to be more memorable. It was a sensible approach to overcome the challenge they had faced previously. You can imagine my surprise when on the display screen I was presented with the word 'CRIPT'. Yes, it accurately presented all the letters of the newly designed values, but as a growing business in the plastics industry– at that time under significant pressure from the press to be sustainable– it just did not work, and that is an understatement. This again shows that planning is key and, when working in a language that is not your mother tongue, it is important to use experts to support your goals and to trust them when they make recommendations that will protect you.

THE MONKEY ON YOUR SHOULDER

In the early 2020s, I was working with a very energised team. A group of like-minded people had almost organically come together and, as a team, we achieved the most amazing results. Building the pipeline was going great guns, and new creative thinking and actions were putting the business and the product on the map! What was lagging behind was the market readiness of the product.

Rightfully, the best person to progress the final designs into production was appointed to pull the team into the final part of the launch phase. At the end of the year, the engineering team had completed their part, so it was back to the sales team to deliver the goods through pre-order conversion.

In a meeting that followed, the project lead commented that the 'monkey' was now transferring to the person taking the lead in the team for sales. When questioning it, I understood that the lead was actually passing a toy monkey around the team to identify who was responsible for delivering the next part of the result. It was unbelievable that, in this day and age, we had not managed to lead with more understanding. It was clear upon this lead joining the team that all team dynamics had changed. Where previously joint values had pushed the team to great heights, we were now confronted with people in the team exhibiting extensive fearful behaviour.

The team started to be managed by reporting and in an old-fashioned way; they were challenging the numbers, rather than starting to understand the drivers in the decision-making process and acting to 'fix' the points that were not aligning with the voice of the customer. The end result was the organic dismantling of the team – the goals at inception were inspirational and visionary, but after a short period of time, the magic had disappeared and with it the opportunity to really maximise the results for the company. Again, this proves that success starts with the lead.

SHHH, IT'S A SECRET

I have worked in quite a few businesses where the financial end result is poorly communicated, or not communicated at all. How is it possible that senior leaders in a business forget to share the goals for the year or for the longer term? Just because day in, day out they are working on this with their teams does not mean that *everybody* in the business is clearly aware of what the goals are. It escapes these leaders that we can only expect people to engage if they understand what is required. In many businesses, we see 'town hall' meetings where the goals are being communicated – often at such a high level that the teams, including the leaders, just do not know how they can contribute. What part do they own and is there some joined-up approach on how to tackle the year ahead?

I can understand it if, when you read this, you say, 'Hey, that's not the case at my place! We are great at communication; we do all these events and this and that.' But I challenge you: do you really know that the messages are correctly received, and that you have a coordinated approach to creating business success? Can you, hand on heart, tell me it needs no improvement? In my experience, only 20% of businesses get their whole team to engage and welcome the discussion, participation and challenges. Can you honestly say that all your team members are putting their hand up without fear of getting it wrong? Think back to the classroom experience. Can you honestly say that you invite the participation of both your extrovert and introvert team members, without penalty? If you do, does everybody participate as equals? In most teams, this is not the case.

MONEY IS THE PURPOSE

How far you have developed as a business– and, more importantly, the development of the team members in your business– can easily be measured by asking your teams this question: what is the purpose of this business? You will be astounded by the answers you collect. The CEO of a business I worked for in the late 2010s actually came out with the quote: 'We are in business to make money and that is our purpose.' Admittedly, the business was not doing well due to lack of ownership of the business challenges, plus a serious amount of over-resourcing and an inability to deal with the underperformers.

They had been 'plain sailing' for years as a disruptor in the market. I take none of their successes away from them.

In the early years, they were groundbreaking. They continued with a good vision, with sustainability at the core of their business model. The challenge they had was that they would not permit themselves to be challenged by their teams – they hired the best of the best, only to ignore them when the 'rubber hit the road' and times got tougher.

I distinctly remember, in a moment of the CEO 'losing it', being told, 'Annemieke, we are here to make money only.' I tried protesting to remind them of the key reasons I joined: clear values and focus on creating 'a better world'. It was then that I was told there is only one reason for business, and that is money.

Of course, I understand the sentiment: if there is no income, there is no business. However, have a look around; if there is no purpose, your user base will not be interested in engaging with you. Today's users are looking for broader engagement; they are looking for you to be doing good; they want to be able to trust your business to do the right thing, to be socially responsible and ethically sustainable. Only then do they 'carry you' to deliver the desired result. I don't only point this out; I actually work with teams delivering this day to day. So, money is what facilitates business, but it should never be its purpose; it should always be the outcome. Many businesses who apply this see great value. A clear example is Patagonia, which is more than just a clothing brand; it's a way of life.

I AM NOT GOOD ENOUGH

You will never hear this from men in business. When I started my new job in the 2010s, I was most surprised to be taken to one side by my new female board member to be confronted with the comment, 'I am really pleased you have joined us, and I am excited about the growth we will be able to achieve with you on board.' I was flattered. We then progressed to discussing what was needed to facilitate this growth. The faster you grow in a manufacturing business, the more capital you will require to 'keep the dream alive'. I was told in no uncertain terms that she did not think she would be able to facilitate the company's growth in the years to come.

In the following years, you could see from the behaviours of the executives that the values displayed were a 'front' and therefore were not experienced by the employees and customers as genuine. And when this creeps in, you get a misalignment of purpose and value, resulting in fearful behaviours; this, if you are lucky, slowly erodes the company and its delivered results. In this case, the company took a nosedive – not only due to this misalignment, but because inexperience, secretive behaviour of the executive, and a pandemic were all at play. There are different perspectives here: the company has survived for now, but it still displays the fearful behaviour that has made it into a shadow of its old self. Where once it used to lead the field, it is now merely following.

HOW TO BAKE A CAKE – WITHOUT THE COOKS

If you catch up with any of your friends, and you discuss going out to a Michelin-starred restaurant, the main focus is generally about the outstanding food and service combination. Many will wax lyrical about the quality and overall achievements. Now, stop and think about how this all came to be for these businesses. They probably started with an amazing idea, were passionate about making it a reality, would not settle for second best, wanted to be creative, decided that they wanted to stand out from the crowd. No doubt there was much, much more, too. Then they had to start to make that a reality; they had to hire the best people and create a rhythm in the way their day was structured. They needed to share experiences, and train and develop each other to be the best they could be. Structure and precision are definitely part of the day, as are hierarchy, dedication and commitment to a common goal supported by joint values.

A business like the one described above, we would all agree, would have to focus on leadership and selecting the best of the best to deliver an outstanding 'picture on a plate' each and every day. Chefs who can produce food at the top of their game require passion, precision, commitment, teamwork and much, much more. Their efforts are rewarded not only by restaurant bookings that are snapped up months in advance, but by the visit of the Michelin auditors. Finally, being granted the three-star award is the ultimate reward for all the hard work that has to go in. This will only be achievable, though, if there is no debilitating fear and a great homogeneous belief in the values you hold together as a team.

So how come, when we apply the same logic to traditional businesses, we often come up against many barriers in being able to achieve the successes that are expected? I speak from experience when I tell you that, in the past, I was brought into a business that was keen to replicate the success of its competitor. I was able to evidence the successes through delivered results. These results included reworking the team, development and training, maximisation of productivity, advanced product positioning, brand development and more – much more.

When I was on board, expectations were high, but the brakes went on right from the start, simply because things were not done in the way they used to be done! There were many protected people in the team, who had been successful in the past but could just not keep up with the new requirements. There was a great debilitating fear of letting go and trusting the team members to do the job they were hired to do. If this does not happen, you do need to make sure that you as a leader have access to a system that will put the team members back on track; be prepared to have the difficult conversations.

Needless to say, we never achieved the successes that could so easily have been delivered. In short, because there was insufficient trust in the team they had built around them, there was also little or no appetite for really discussing performance with any of the team members for fear of them leaving – not realising that some were doing their business maximisation potentials a great deal of harm. In fact, they should have left years earlier. Additionally, there was also limited vision on what a global business should look like. Being successful in Europe, the Middle East and Africa does not mean that you can replicate this success in all corners of the world, if you believe that your truth is the only truth. Here you do need intersectionality, so you are able to be at your most creative. To summarise: if you are being asked to bake a cake, make sure they allow you to hire the right team of cooks.

MINI VS ROLLS ROYCE

Today I was reminded about a subject we used to discuss extensively as a team. The sales team is always keen to win, which generally means winning the deal. Often, however, they do not. The win is not forthcoming because they do not put the work in. The win is not delivered because the team is working to offer the most comprehensive solution to the customer, fully missing the customer's driver to maximise value. Now, of course, I will be simplifying the issue here, as the selection of a provider (product or service) is much more complex than I can describe at this point, but bear with me. The point I am trying to put across is that we would do well to use the car dealer principle. First, they get you hooked on owning that particular car. Then, once you are on the hook, you will be reeled in with extras that you just simply cannot do without. Recognise this strategy.

When we are working in our business, do we forget these simple strategies that we are submitted to every day in our personal life? Where they work? Or do we not think they have made a big impact, or that they could not even be applied to situations in our business life?

When working with groups, I used to work with them on the Mini analogy. Offer the customer the base model of your product or services. This will ensure that you are 'matched up' to your competitor. Then start to build the product/service to the client's additional needs, and make sure that you put the effort in to explain what they will receive in addition while spending this extra cash. They are not mind readers, nor do they have a crystal ball. If there is something so special that it will further revolutionise the offering, you have to take the time to explain it. Make sure to add it in the last section, highlight the extra gains and the overall delivered results. This, I call the 'Mini–Rolls Royce option': from the basic model to the best of the best. You have to be engaged here to be the best of the best; take a shortcut here– or worse, be lazy– and you will lose.

It is interesting: the salesperson will fear the loss of the deal and will take shortcuts to try to secure the contract. They offer the 'Rolls Royce' option much too early in the game, often right at the start. This is due to the flawed belief that the customer always wants to buy the best. In doing so, they lose the connection with their audience very quickly, as the decision-maker is only interested in finding the best fit for the most competitive price. The reason for this positioning is that they fear making the wrong decision. The choice needs to be able to be held up against the light and stand up to scrutiny, plus the values that the organisation holds dear. But believe you me, the decision-maker's actions will be driven by fear much more than they are driven by their overall values, both personal and business.

NEW INVESTOR INTRODUCTION

A few years ago, I was introduced to a possible new investor in the business. Securing this investment was key to the short- and possibly long-term future of the company. Unexpectedly, I found myself in the same place as the investor, and my peers decided that it would be brilliant for them to meet with me. Without any brief, I attended the meeting. Interestingly, I was asked to attend at 11am, and was punctually on time after completely changing my diary to accommodate the request, only to be waved away that they were not ready yet. Then I was asked to return promptly at 12 noon.

More diary rearranging. When we finally met, it was very clear that they were working to a very old-fashioned activity input system for sales. 'How do you manage your team?' and 'How many phone calls do they make?' was the extent of the conversation. They also expected a presentation– my peers had never informed me of this. This left me with the feeling that I had been set up. Soon after, an interim project manager was appointed. As you would expect, they were collecting all data relevant to the business, following which they were able to restructure. Needless to say, my values did not align with their business, and we parted ways. It's interesting to note that the business is still in heavy seas.

TRADITION

This was in the early 2000s. Tired of working 24/7 in a pressurised role in the City of London, I was offered a role in the Midlands.

So keen was I to change that I looked at everything through rose-tinted glasses. Previously, I had worked in an environment driven by Montblanc pens and sharp suits. I did feel at home there and I was very successful, but I was also keen to achieve more.

After a rigorous selection process, I accepted the new role. On day one I parked in the designated parking spot, only to be pursued by the parking attendant with the message that 'This is for directors'. I was one of them, a woman. All parked up, I walked into the building for my first day only to find that dress-down Monday was my start day. Tracksuits and trainers were all around me.

The board met once a month in the boardroom, at a green felt table with the obligatory tea and coffee service.

Needless to say, I delivered the required result... and then found a new tribe that more accurately matched my values. I am very pleased to have had the experience, though, as my selection process has now also been adjusted as a result.

MY STORIES – LIFE

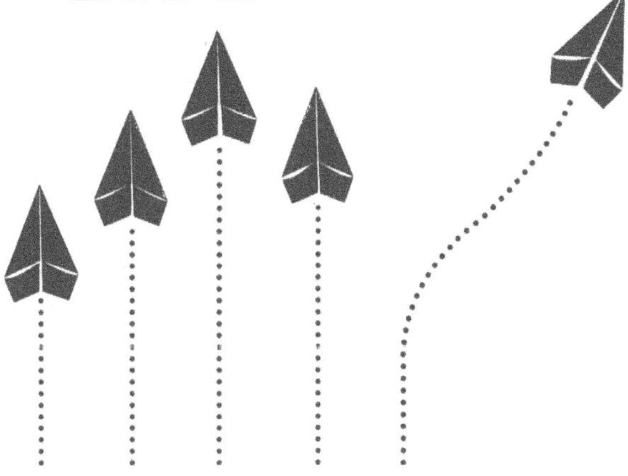

PERSONAL

We all start with nothing, and we ultimately leave with nothing. How we choose to spend the time in between is up to us. Yet in your twenties, thirties and forties, it just does not seem that way. People from my generation are caught in the never-ending circle of work. Some have lifted work to some 'higher being'-like status, and I was one of them.

Let me just give you a snippet of my life prior to turning 55. It may sound familiar to some of you.

I was a high-flying executive – quite literally. I travelled for 80% of my working life – and yes, I did have a BA gold card. I had operated as chief commercial officer and at board level for over 15 years. I was hooked on being busy and successful. I used my time when travelling for work; this means meetings during the working hours 08:00–18:00 and then spending the evenings catching up on emails, projects and other work stuff. I can truly say that I managed to cram two years' work into one, and I was proud to be able to do so. I was delivering value! Writing this down now… wow, it offers me a great opportunity to reflect. No judgement, but truly reflecting.

Many of us are working towards or through serious burnout. The outline above shows how it happens with the best of intentions. It either happens consciously (although you are not able to stop it happening) or subconsciously (in which case, a nasty surprise awaits you).

Many of us look towards work to give their life meaning – work is purpose. For some of us, work is a hobby, something we do because it brings us joy and great satisfaction. I am also aware that some of those whose hobby has become their work are now so busy delivering that they are starting to hate exactly the thing they used to love; it is such a shame. I am aware, too, that some have stopped these kinds of jobs, so they are able to enjoy their hobby as just that: a hobby to be enjoyed.

For many, work is a means to an end. And I am also aware that for many a job is necessary to maintain a lifestyle. Bills, commitments, schooling of children and more – all of it requires a certain income level. Once you are on the treadmill, it is difficult to get off without leaving a trail of disaster in your wake. Deep breaths, and keep calm and carry on!

Here, I would like to set out what is happening to many of us. I was caught in this circle for years. I loved my job and found it fulfilling. In addition to work giving my life meaning, I also got caught up in the material security that made me fearful of losing the life I had created for myself. It was that never-ending circle of working to live: buying a big house, and then working to keep living in the big house.

To most people around me, I had the best jobs, always travelling, racking up the air miles (while never having the time to spend them), visiting a new place each day, exploring cultures and seeing new things; it was all part of the job. In addition, I was also presented with a great opportunity to indulge in my hobby, photography, while travelling – but in the early days of my work, I never had time for anything other than airports, meetings and work, let alone taking some pictures.

Before you knew it, I too was caught in the vortex; sucked into the bigger job, bigger house, larger-than-life living; it was always bigger and better for everything. Yes, I did secure it and financially sustained it (with many a hairy moment in all of those years). At some point, however, your life changes. There are choices to be made.

Retaining this life could mean compromising values for your work! If you don't do this, you may lose everything you have built up. Is that the person you want to be? Each and every one of you will ask yourselves this question, often with different outcomes; even different days would get me to respond with a different answer.

Slowly, and only in the last five years (yep, after age 50!), I started to carve out time for myself on these trips, only after one of my team members had a stern talk to me about lifestyle. I was told to go find a restaurant and see something of the local area, take some pictures! Life is short, so go live it!

If you ask me, it was worth it. Yes, I have certainly compromised– a lot– as I have managed to convince myself that the situation demanded the compromise. But don't we all do this? Upon reflection, I have no regrets, and on balance, I would say that I have always been fair and kind to others.

When asking myself the question, was it from time to time driven by fear? Well, absolutely. Could the situation have been dealt with differently? No doubt. We all know hindsight is a wonderful thing. And as I set out before, on balance, it was the right thing to do for me at the time.

Why do we look at situations differently when we get older? Maybe we have achieved everything in life and there is time to change to a different life. In my situation, what I had least feared came about (my relationship, which I had considered to be rock solid, fell apart). Then the thing I most feared happened shortly after: I lost my job, with the accompanying loss of earnings.

How do we end up at that point? And more importantly, how do we take control?

RESOURCE PACK

Now is a good moment for you to reflect on the fear that may hold you back. Take some time to think about your values. Are they clear and well defined, and are you able to maximise your potential?

Is fear, deep down, holding you back?

You can access the Resource Pack here:

www.annemiekehartmanjemmett.com

In the Resource Pack you will find a postcard on which you can write down the fear(s) that is holding you back.

THE PLAYGROUND – DON'T ASSUME

CHALLENGE

They know what I mean, so I can assume a whole bunch of things, and this will get us to the end result more quickly.

MY STORY

Successful communications are at the heart of monetising commercial situations. The building of trust is at the core of doing deals. The only way of building trust is through the creation of joint understanding – the kind of understanding that means you both see the same picture; you walk the same path, travel the same road. Very often, this is not the case, and we take too many shortcuts too often and too early. We assume that the recipient 'knows', don't they? Let's move more quickly – it is about delivering the result.

When I say this to people, the response often is: of course they know what I mean – they were in the same place, or they have also experienced it. This makes us all lazy in our approach. Here is a really good example to illustrate what I mean. And this is exactly at the core of why things go wrong or why we misunderstand.

I use the 'playground at school' analogy frequently when working with teams. Let me give you some insight into this, so that we are starting at the same point. In conversations, we often use the same words to explain something and/or share information. So how is it possible for all those misunderstandings to take place? Quite simply, because with the use of the same words, we may all understand the setting, but our viewpoints and experiences are different; in short, we all see a different picture.

Here is some more detail to explain the essence and to create true understanding of what I mean.

We have all been to school (this is an assumption, but in 99.9% of cases a correct one; if you are inquisitive enough at this stage, you will filter out the 0.1% that has not been to school). So let's work on the premise that in Europe at least, we can all relate to school times. Is the assumption correct that, if I want to start explaining something, I can start straight away with the belief that everybody in my audience can see the same picture as me of the playground at school? Can I allow myself to 'shortcut' here, to move forward with further detail and expect everybody to take away the same details? Many of you would respond here by saying, 'Yes, just go ahead – I can see the playground at school.' I would agree that everybody who has been to school and played in the playground has a common understanding of what it looked like, at least in outline.

To jump ahead at this stage, however, and progress to the key points that you would like to explain would be similar to building a house without foundations.

The key to this is that, prior to moving forward, we align all our experiences: we make sure that we see the individual detail in the picture. After years of experience and asking people the fine detail about their playgrounds at school, I have come to know that, unless I have attended the same school at the same time as the person I am working or talking with, it is 100% certain that I will *not* have the same detail in my mental picture as the other person has in theirs when we talk about school playgrounds. So let me go into a bit more detail here.

When I was at junior school, the school playground was very open and, in addition to a tiled play area, we also had a huge (or at least it seemed huge when I was four) sandpit with a concrete rim. The sandpit was completely surrounded by big concrete boulders that were cemented together. 'How is this relevant?' you ask. Well, you will find out shortly...

In addition to all of the above, we also had access to a metal 'pull buggy'. This was great fun and enhanced our play time. This detail is of key importance in my life – but only for one reason. One day when I was playing, my finger was trapped between the metal buggy and the concrete retaining boulder. This did indeed scar my hand for life – but I lived and was an experience richer. Plus, I now know that my hand should steer well away from metal buggies, edges and concrete environments! It hurt, a lot!

Other details are that the playground butted directly onto the football pitches, which were great open grassy areas– excellent for play in the summer but not during the winter, when they were flooded to make sure that we had a safe ice-skating area when the frost set in. I grew up in Holland, remember. With this information, even when you have been to the same school at the same time, to see the same aligned image, it would be good to ask which period you are talking about (summer/winter), which country you were in (as the picture may look very different at different parts of the year) and to take different cultures into consideration.

Maybe take three minutes of your time now and envisage your own playground at the school you attended between the ages of 4 and 11. I bet you that even the two playgrounds for your junior and senior schools were different. No doubt your junior school playground was very different from mine... and even if it was the same, hopefully you did not scar any body parts for life.

The outline above aims to highlight that when we work with others or share experiences, to create a common understanding we need to start by really seeing the same picture. We need to calibrate and align and clearly define what the starting point is. The base level needs to be well defined. Just like the house, it needs strong foundations from which we can start to build the most amazing and resilient houses. A weak foundation may be good enough to build a shed that may stay upright for a long period of time. But if you have aspirations that may take many years to deliver to their full potential, I propose that you do the groundwork first. The playground analogy is a great way for us to communicate that using the same words is not the same as creating a common understanding. Very simply, communication rather than assumption will put you in the driving seat.

You may want to know how I came to find this out. For years, I have been attending meetings that involve both English and Dutch speakers. On the face of it, they get on and understand each other. They have a western European, cold-weather approach to life and, even though the English don't speak Dutch, seemingly it is easy for them to understand each other: they all speak English.

As per the standard English response, the Dutch speak such great English! If you are the one, however, who understands the pictures of the Dutch person *and* the English person, you will frequently come across events where they both use the same words, but they definitely *do not* mean the same thing. In general, this is not a major disaster, as oblivion in most cases is not a major impairment to being understood. It can pass for both parties without any real in-depth explanation being required.

Yet, when it comes to contracts and the true meaning of what is being agreed, often you will be presented with unexpected surprises. Now that you have this extra piece of knowledge, it would be very interesting to put it to the test; 'maybe sooner than when your life depends on it' would be my recommendation.

In summary: communicate and ask questions, do not assume – this is so you can create a common ground and understanding from which you will achieve your goals more quickly.

TAKE CONTROL

- **Fear**: Additional information will offer greater insight and understanding. It also shows that others have had a life, and that this life may not always have been without challenge. It makes others more human; it allows you to see the person rather than the picture of perfection they may share and that you have created for them in your mind.

- **Trust**: This way of engaging makes everybody a real person. It allows you to have empathy and builds strong bonds among all participants. This ultimately allows you to deliver to your joint outcomes in a harmonious way. Ultimately, taking the time will get you to move accurately to the required end goal. By taking time at the outset, you will be well positioned to move more quickly throughout the task. Creating good understanding early on, and building trust, sees the whole process become more enjoyable, offering autonomy to all.

- **Values**: Through engagement and learning more, you start to see the values shine through while sharing stories on a common subject or event. This creates understanding and communality. Others will now *really* know what is meant, and no assumptions need to be made; you will achieve accuracy in the detail.

SCHOOL DYNAMICS – ASKING QUESTIONS PUTS YOU AHEAD

CHALLENGE

Asking questions makes you sound stupid. Responding to questions makes you a clever-clogs.

MY STORY

Who would have thought that you can never really escape the school dynamic unless you really understand this? Our formative years happen both at school and at home. I would like to highlight a commonality that we are all presented with, 100%, no matter which country we have been educated in.

When attending classes, participation is highly appreciated, and it is how we learn – and how we maximise engagement! We all recall attending class and no doubt dreading the moment the teacher asks a question. If you know the answer with 100% certainty, you are in the money! Your arm goes up and you are ready to answer the question. Frequently, however, we are uncertain of the answer to the question, so we hide – and hope that somebody else gets to be spotlighted! Recognise the event, feel the anxiety.

I was particularly reluctant to participate in maths (my dad was a maths teacher, so by definition– or so I had convinced myself– I would not understand the detail). Another rather awkward element was that I was shy when I was young. If unsure, although I was needing to respond, I would go bright red. Not a great look, which earned me the nickname 'Tomato' for a while. Innocent? Yes. High-impact at the time? Absolutely. Was I likely to respond when unsure? Absolutely not.

We will push a little further. What about when you don't know something during class? Do you let it pass, deciding to research it later? Or, bravest of all, do you raise your hand to ask a question? Most of us choose to ask the question only once we have evaluated the following: do I sound dumb by asking? Once you're sure the answer is no, then and only then do you raise your hand.

The above detail is a great example of how we are conditioned to behave. Early on, we decide how we present: a follower or a leader, in the background or out front with chutzpah. Now we get to the workplace, where there is not just the class dynamic at play. Here we can lose our livelihood by sounding ill-prepared, stupid, not worthy and all those things that we have decided to believe about ourselves. So, many people just do the minimum; they make sure they do not get noticed. Does this mean you get the best out of your teams? You absolutely, and with confidence, do *not*.

As leaders we need to understand the dynamic of what is happening in all of these moments. Bring it back to fear, trust and values. The leader needs to create an environment where individuals feel safe, in both team settings and 'Lone Ranger' situations. Behaviour based on values can only be observed when there is a safe space, where questions can be asked without judgement and patient in-depth responses bring people on the journey. They can try things out, fail without judgement and get up and try again. The creation of the safe space is the leader's responsibility and *must* be protected. It is the only way that fear can be held at bay; if the fear creeps in, you will start to get the team and individual performance falling apart.

This does not mean you cannot manage the team to performance indicators – no, you absolutely can – but you have to set out the rules of the game early and explain that you expect them to fail and learn from each event. Make the mistake once, the blame is on the 'teacher'; fail twice, blame on the 'student' – address it and move on.

SIDELINE EXPERTS

No doubt you have come across these team members. They have a great skill (or so they believe): they can point out with laser precision what is going wrong! They would be the people in the class who change the subject all the time because they want to stay 'top dog'.

In some ways they are valuable, as they are successful in highlighting what needs addressing. To only see them as an irritant would not help your cause at all. But if you give them space without restrictions, you run the risk of turning off team members who are expressing and adhering to the values you have agreed to as a team. So, what to do?

In practice, and from experience, the way to engage them is to agree a methodology early on. You invite them to knock themselves out in identifying the issues – you want to improve as a team and a business, so people with a critical eye are valuable. To ensure good engagement, adherence to the agreed values and the reduction of fearful behaviour, you add two additional rules to the identification game. In addition to only pointing out what is wrong, you invite them to add what *they* will do to support the fix and you ask who *they need* to help create the fix.

This is a really easy way to invite engagement across the team, for all team members to be vigilant in identifying improvement opportunities, while prompting active requesting of participation from the identifier as well as the team members.

Improvement Opportunities + Identifier + Team Members = Values-Based Teamwork

TAKE CONTROL

- **Fear:** Create a safe space. This can be the leader or the team member taking the initiative; promote engagement and the asking of questions. The more you do so, the easier it gets. Confidence will increase and comfort will start to develop over time. Challenging each other starts to be constructive rather than destructive.

- **Trust:** This approach creates trust. Openly discussing challenges, sharing insecurities, improving understanding... they all work on creating trust, which in turn offers transparency and openness. This generates good engagement and participation.

- **Values:** By acting in this way, teams will start to share their values as individuals and as a team.

TEAMS – SETTING GOALS GIVES CLARITY TO ALL

CHALLENGE

Let's do it my way. I do things perfectly well, why do others not do it the same way?

MY STORY

Remember those days when you were part of a team? Football, netball, softball, rugby, cycling… Not only is it great fun to be part of the team, think of the parties after the win! Or the commiseration! All offer the opportunity to bond us in a sound way. I loved playing team sports.

In the creation of a team, as outlined above, we seemingly believe that it is easy to plan and have a joint goal. Instinctively, we know that when we are a cohesive unit, we are most likely to successfully achieve these goals. In the planning phase, we are really good at defining who is responsible for what. Just imagine back to those sports days– the cries of, 'We will win 5–0!' This optimism and the numbers-defined goal clearly communicate the planned result, in a measurable way.

Now, go back into project and work mode. I was reminded of the elements required for teams to be successful during a recent conversation. This is important enough that I will outline it here for you to be able to reflect and bring your own nuances to this overview.

Often when working in teams we are disappointed and get frustrated. The reason for the frustration is that others do not do things in quite the way we want them to; our way is best! For example, the submission deadlines are missed, or work is returned with short-notice turnaround times, or the quality of work is disappointing and the overall submission lacks cohesion.

Stop and think! How much time do we really spend at the start aligning our team? As you can see from many years of watching *The Apprentice* or participating in contests, people automatically just want to get stuck in. They are conditioned that way. Never mind the critical 'getting on the same page' investment of time. The key is often, 'let's get moving – we will figure it out along the way'.

If, from the outset, we spend only five minutes establishing what we are aiming for, we are more likely to get a much-improved result, as per the 5–0 win goal in the earlier example. Establish with your teams what the outcome needs to be. Use a number. Discuss among yourselves: What would be OK for us all? What are we all going for? A 6 out of 10? Or are there members in your team keen to deliver amazing work worthy of 9 out of 10? Here you need to negotiate and create buy-in. Get agreement on the quality of work that you are aiming to deliver so you start aligned. By doing this, you have created a 'hook': a point of agreement and clarity which is so significantly important that you can bring situations and events back to this moment of agreement when events go off track. It is easy to give it a result number, and it offers clarity to all about what you are aiming for and what you are committing to.

The next step is to agree a contract with each other. Contracting in this context means getting agreement as to how you will work to deliver the project. Submission deadlines should be discussed, also time available for reworks etc.

Once you have this very simple framework in place, you can 'call each other out' on the agreements you have made. For instance, you have all agreed that the quality of work you should be aiming to submit is 8 out of 10 (so good and will stand up to scrutiny), you will submit final copy seven days before the deadline, the turnaround of submitted work to the group for review by the project manager should be within 24 hours. Excellent. Now you have all the details in place to challenge if things go off track.

A member of your team delivers poor-quality work – the eyes of the group then ask an open question: do you think this submission will get us the 8 out of 10 that we agreed to deliver from the outset? If no, then explore how, together, you can deliver an improved version. In case the answer is yes, then bring to the team's attention the areas where you think the submission is on shaky ground – be specific and supportive. Agree together how you will improve to deliver to the target of delivering work worthy of 8 marks out of 10.

You get the point, no doubt. And it's the same with the submission date, if you have agreed this as a group and all have signed off on it. When submissions are late, call each other out on it. Find out why. Again, be supportive and always have an open mind. In general, team members do not set out to boycott the process or the project, so listen – yes, really listen – to what has happened in their life to have caused it to go off track.

TAKE CONTROL

- **Fear:** As you see, creating the framework from the outset offers clarity. It gets you all to push off from the same point at the same time with clear and joint understanding. Taking five minutes to sort this out from the start will save you hours of frustration, misunderstanding and ultimately poor results. Take ownership and get the results you deserve. Here there is no place for fear, of conflict, lack of control and more.
- **Trust:** Because you now have clarity, you have created 'hooks' to which you can bring the conversation back – you all agreed. You quickly create trust and a common goal.
- **Values:** By taking this approach, you align the values of the group, creating synergy.

INSPIRATIONAL LEADER – THERE IS A PERSON BEHIND THE FAÇADE

CHALLENGE

Showing up as I am or as people expect me to be.

MY STORY

When we are children, the conversation around the dinner table is often about what we want to be 'when we grow up'. Initially, the conversation for me was all about what I would enjoy and, maybe even more importantly, how I could earn a living from what I enjoyed doing. Remember, this is something that you have to get out of bed for each morning!

This starts early, often at school. My initial ideas, as an active teenager, were all about the outdoors, performance and doing the right thing. School subjects were not really of interest; a poor history teacher who was more into the 'tissues that needed to be deposited in the waste bin' (hygiene pre-pandemic) than teaching us why history has an impact on how we live our lives today did not set me off to a good start. Sadly, it is all I remember from my history lessons.

I had a brilliant French teacher (she was Belgian) who allowed me to submit a French project late to incorporate my visit to Paris – genius; but the one that followed had a real chip on her shoulder and could not inspire. I never regained my enthusiasm for the language in quite the same way.

The Dutch teachers had no chance with me. Why speak Dutch? It is complicated, with words ending in d, t or dt all dependent on grammar. What is the point? It all sounds the same and nobody speaks Dutch (not quite true: Dutch, Belgian and South African people all speak it or versions of it). But still, to me the whole thing was pointless. In a more measured way, I do know that the ability to speak Dutch is the foundation of the ability to speak other languages well; for instance, German.

If things were not fun, I would move on – quite literally. Not possible at school, but definitely possible afterwards. The only interesting thing at school for me was English, as being able to command the English language allowed me to travel the world, make money and most importantly have fun. Plus, Physical Education, which was outdoors and included ice-skating in the winter, was great! Additionally, there were opportunities to win races on that 'flooded football pitch' outside of my junior school playground. As you may remember, fun was one of my previous values.

This was supposed to be a chapter on inspirational leadership. How could the school things be relevant? In reviewing and starting to write, it has become clear to me that from a young age you start to observe how people interact. Well, at least, I did. The French teachers are a really good example. The Belgian lady I would have followed anywhere; the Dutch French teacher with an obsession about France not so much. The chip on her shoulder also did not help with her likability. Not that you necessarily need to like people to be able to engage, but it does help.

Back to making a choice on my career. My decision at a very early stage was to join the police service. It balanced well with the active lifestyle, career opportunities, long-term life prospects and overall security it offered, the pensions and other 'facilities'. In the early days pondering this, it was a real contender– possibly the only contender, if I am honest. In researching this, and with six A-levels banked, it was clear it was not in line with the entry criteria to attend the police academy; it was much more likely that I would join as a bobby on the beat. Nothing wrong with that, but not really what I had envisaged in my mind's eye or in line with my parents' expectations, if I am really truthful. It also meant that I would have to put myself at risk, a lot – or so I had decided – and work hard to make my way up the chain. This was not a great long-term strategy, I decided. In essence, it boiled down to the ability to have fun.

The search continued. After a few twists and turns, I settled on a course of study in hospitality management (including economics, law, administration, languages, nutrition and more). What made me settle on this route? Well, you could easily combine a number of my key 'fun' elements, including communication (marketing, people management, guests and service) and travel (jobs are available all around the world), and a key differentiator was that I could start in year two (I was allowed to take years one and two in one year), which meant that I would be in the school benches for one year, go out to the wide world for an internship year in year three, and finalise in year four with an exam year. Deal! I joined. Ultimately, it also proved to be a great base from which to secure a sound commercial and board career.

IHG INTERCONTINENTAL – HOLIDAY INN

In my third year at college, I managed to secure an internship abroad with the IHG Group of hotels and selected Birmingham, UK, of all places. In the 80s this was the place to be, as the 'New Romantics' were ruling the airwaves, so life outside of work was interesting to say the least. At work it was fabulous, as I was quite an exotic colleague. From Holland, prepared to work hard, good in engagement and ready to roll up my sleeves to help out. This is also where leadership started to present itself across the 'managers'. Some played by the rules, which was rather boring but respected. Others took a different approach and managed to get even better engagement by delivering amazing results, but they did stretch the rules a bit. I remember one of the managers fondly. They were responsible for banqueting and events.

We used to work hard looking after the guests. The team was made up of youngsters and a group of older (much older) waitresses of almost or beyond retirement age. The older ladies – yes, they were all ladies – used to be very happy looking after tables post-pudding service. The younger crew would then 'nip out' under the guidance of the banqueting manager to go and see many of the bands that were playing in the local Odeon; they were often guests of the hotel and therefore there was an abundance of free tickets available. It was only for a maximum of 30 minutes that we would attend the concerts, but it was such a buzz and such leadership from the manager that the team was 'ready to die for him' at any moment.

In this unique team, we were playfully taught that we all had a duty to look after each other, help and support where possible, engage to show up as our best self and teach others what we know. (I have taught many people how to perform silver service – a great skill to this day!) We also learned that rules are there as a guide; respect others, but do not blindly follow – take the opportunity when it presents itself, but always, always look out for each other. This applied whether you were the boss or one of the team members. It was the best learning experience I could have had. And we always turned in an excellent performance, with sales results well above those of other teams.

The years that followed were quite tame by comparison. I worked in every department in the hotel. But none offered the relative freedom we experienced in those early years. Additionally, the banqueting department also lends itself to this way of working. You can plan and predict, being in the limelight for part of the day and in the back office for the rest.

Years later, I managed my own teams. We applied a lot of the learning that I had experienced in my early days. I was strict but fair – and we had a lot of fun, all while exploring, learning and developing together. The education in those days, as part of the job, was still excellent – so the company received a lot of things in return, from commitment to significant increases in revenue. This was my speciality to make sure that I could run my own show.

How did I do it? I soon figured out that you need to think creatively if you want to increase revenue with 100% occupancy. In the banqueting area this means upselling and education; menu choices and wine selections were critical to our success, as was selling rooms more than once a day. This sounds standard in this day and age, but in our day it was revolutionary.

How did I become a leader rather than a manager? In those early days, I just did what felt right. And, maybe due to my upbringing – my father was a headmaster – I felt the need to teach, train and develop. I have also managed to start to listen intently from a very early stage; people give you every clue you need! They tell you how they can turn in the best performance each day and all you need to do is pay attention and *listen*. Leadership, in my mind, really is not that difficult.

Maybe I think this way because ego, for me, does not feature. My team's success reflects positively on me; I just need to facilitate and create the environment, and the rest takes care of itself. In the early days, that is exactly how it happened. To finish up on my hospitality days, one year I was managing a big team, which was still in the UK but no longer in Birmingham. We were working in December. Yes, you guessed it: Christmas parties from 3rd December. By the time everybody got a break from Christmas the team were like dead men walking! How could you motivate them? It used to be customary for the team to be presented with tips at the end of the Christmas period. In those days, you could walk off with a significant amount of extra pay. Prior to the month of December, we agreed how we were going to turn in our best performance each day, what would keep us motivated and how we could survive the onslaught.

Three options were discussed: take the money, run and go drinking; go to Alton Towers and let your hair down; or get waited on hand and foot with dinner at the Ritz in London. The choice was the team's. Clearly, prior to the choice being made, it was my responsibility to set out the options. As part of this, it was also my responsibility to set out what could be gained from each:

- Option 1: Yes, you could reward yourself with something that you had your eye on. Great for a short-term injection of motivation.
- Option 2: A great day out, some team-building, lots of drink would likely be involved and a great time would be had by all.
- Option 3: Great fun in booking it, anticipating what it would be like; it offered a comparison between how we expressed service at IHG and how they did so at the Ritz. This was a learning experience– and most importantly it was possibly the only option that offered the opportunity to tell your grandkids about the amazing experience you had.

What choice did the team make? Yes, of course, there was never any doubt about it. They chose option 3.

Let's pick this apart and look at leadership retrospectively. A leader sets the scene and offers options and insights; the choice is always up to the team. On occasion, they may make a choice that, however well set up, might surprise you. The important part is that you should let it happen, let the team make the choices that are right for them, create a safe space around them so that they can 'fall' but also recover. We learn more from the things that go wrong than from the times when everything is protected and goes to plan. The main thing is that it is discussed and there is a learning. It is our responsibility as leaders to support, develop, train and guide. And yes, sometimes that also means guiding people out of the job. I have learned that it takes two to tango. It is the leader's responsibility to create the right environment and support through sharing knowledge, facilitating learning and much more; there is, however, a responsibility on the team members to engage, challenge, ask and implement. If there is no joint engagement, the partnership is doomed to fail.

OTHER EXPERIENCES

Over the years I have worked with many different teams, in global cultural settings and in very diverse businesses. There are many similar stories to be told across the years – in fact, enough for a few books. There is a common thread across all of these teams and businesses. We work with humans, and humans have the same key drivers that bring unity. Treat people with respect. Sometimes this means as a leader you need to educate yourself on how to get the best out of individuals and members of a team (they can be very different, so take time to find out about your unconscious biases – rest assured you have them – and be aware of them).

Understanding what the individuals within your team fear most is key to building a secure team. Be genuinely interested in what motivates them each and every day, understand their personal situations, be clear in communicating what you expect, show them the route – what is the team looking to achieve and why? Work on values with the team, let the team define how these values touch them, how they can own them and (most importantly) how they can behave to express their values.

Mix this up, and you will never have a structural issue with fear driving the team and the people in it. Values and trust will drive the team. It will not be an easy ride as a leader, as it will require constant adjustment, guidance and attention – again, we are all humans and have a great tendency to go off course.

TAKE CONTROL

- **Fear:** Take the time and have a real interest in people. Respect their views. It is likely that they are different to your own, and that is OK. It will generate understanding and create common ground. This process will also create respect. There is a person behind the presenting person, so find out who they really are. You don't need to agree on everything; seeing the other person's viewpoint is often sufficient to create a common understanding and move forward from there.
- **Trust:** Getting to know each other, creating respect and understanding, builds trust, but this can take time, so invest and explore.
- **Values:** In sharing, you start to become aware of each other's values, and this creates good understanding and commonality. You can build from here, making the relationship stronger.

VOODOO OR MORE

CHALLENGE

Not all learning is linear.

MY STORY

As you have figured out by now, my journey has not been completely linear. Events have presented themselves throughout my working life, and many have been completely unexpected. By going with the flow, and saying yes often, I have come across the most interesting insights.

As I have outlined already, I am interested in language and even more interested in communication. When a few years ago I was asked to help a friend in assessing her hypnotherapy course (yes, really), I did not hesitate in saying yes. Key for her was to understand how the course was structured, to review the teaching styles and to understand overall participation. This needed a commitment from me of 14 weekends, but hey, why not? I was intrigued and interested in the subject. I would take the course as one of the group's participants and would end up with a certificate at the culmination of the course, and could become a practitioner.

I was always interested in the conscious mind and the unconscious (or subconscious) mind, and this offered me amazing perspectives. I learned a lot and did give excellent feedback. OMG, how interesting! Advertisers are masters of creating longing and belonging in this way.

And, although I do not practise hypnotherapy today (or ever, other than in the study environment), I use the learning in my daily life each and every day. If you are interested in exploring this, read up on waking hypnosis. Dr Tim Brunson and Bryan Westra are good authors to start with if you want to know more.

Learning about the power of words, the selection of words to use and how to communicate in a way that links to the outcome you are looking to achieve gave me an extremely powerful insight. I am confident that this skill is an extra contributor to my success today.

Fear is often generated by the lack of consideration and selection of words by the leaders in business. Often it is totally unnecessary for team members to feel threatened, and this can be avoided if more care is taken in the choice of words used. Once we find importance in joint values, the words are easier to find in creating understanding and generating security in the person's position in the situation, company or team.

Is hypnotherapy voodoo or a great skill to have? In my opinion, it is a great skill to have if you understand the impact of words on the conscious and unconscious (subconscious) mind, using it with care and respect. If used with malicious intent, then many would say it is more akin to voodoo – so I am always responsible in its application.

TAKE CONTROL

- **Fear**: Broaden your horizons, understand more of what is around you. It will enrich your life and generate additional engagement.
- **Trust:** Understanding the conscious and unconscious mind will allow you to be much more aware, and this in turn will offer deep understanding and awareness, generating trust through communication.
- **Values:** You will notice that a shift of acceptance will take place. You will start to be open to others' diverse views and backgrounds. You will be able to progress to intersectionality, and this will greatly enhance your ability to be creative in business and life.

COMING OUT – WE ARE ALL THE SAME

CHALLENGE

Showing vulnerability is weak and will not add value to being seen as a leader.

MY STORY

This is probably the most personal story and reference in the book. Part of me thinks that it is really not relevant, as I am no different to the next person, really. But when I stop and reflect, this is possibly the most genuine 'thing' that is key to me being *me*, on all fronts.

Remember this personal story starts over 50 years ago– half a century. The world was different then. The belief at that time was that to 'achieve', you needed to 'fit in'. The more different you were, the fewer opportunities there were. Upon reflection, this is not quite true, of course. Think about some great icons of that era – Vivienne Westwood, Johnny Rotten, David Bowie and many more – they made their uniqueness work for them.

I grew up in a close, loving family, where working hard, being diligent and remaining honest were all valued, and we held the belief that these ideas offered the greatest access to opportunity. Education and kindness to others were the cornerstones of my childhood. The more you 'fitted in' to society, the 'easier' life would be. I totally understand the desire for a parent to offer their child a route to the best 'life'. That is exactly how I started out. A small town, where everybody knew our family, where kindergarten and junior school were a stone's throw away. It was a safe and engaging childhood. I was lucky and I am lucky to have started out in life with this privileged position.

Off I went to senior school, away from the close geographical location to our family home. I was exposed to different influences. And different people. Puberty was another element in the overall mix of growing up. The need to 'fit in' did feature high on the agenda– so I did, for about 10 years. I completed my education, was offered fabulous opportunities and started to build my career. I found out I was pretty good at leadership and delivered great results at work. I was in 'heterosexual relationships' – some look that way now, upon closer refection. These relationships were OK, but something was missing.

I will save you all the detail in the lead-up, but at the age of 25 I decided that I was 'different' and came out. My life was going to be spent with a partner of the same sex, not in the then standard man/woman/two children family make-up that might have given me an easier ride from the outside world. There is a lot of detail I could include here on the journey, but maybe I will keep that for another book.

Here, I started my L life within the LGBTQIA community. For years (and yes, I do mean years), I did not believe that this part of me was relevant in the work setting. Now, I understand that presenting all of me to the outside world in every setting is of key importance.

Referring back to my values– authenticity, inquisitiveness, pleasure, simplicity and creativity– it is key that I do this justice by showing up as a complete person. I have over the years actively participated in events organised by the UHLALA Group and, through this group, I have realised that I need to speak up and show up fully and in full view. It is really important for young people in my community to see that there are no limitations to what they can achieve, regardless of who they choose to share their life with. Although who I choose to spend my life with, in my personal life, is not relevant to others, it is such a key part of who I am and key to my story – my authentic self. I need to show my vulnerability to show my strength.

Now, I also realise that who I am at work and at home has everything to do with the fact that I am gay. My values speak volumes in underlining this statement. It also is a contributing factor, I believe, that I am really and genuinely able to 'tune in' to another person and have empathy. I believe this is one of the key reasons why I have been so successful in life, both in regard to my private life and in business. The ability to listen is a gift, to me and to others.

Times have changed, and on reflection the L in LGBTQIA is pretty mainstream – or so I was told the other day. I now also realise that we need to show up as a group that still needs support; I am shocked daily by how often people in this community are discriminated against. Yes, I know this could start off a full debate, and there are many sides to this story, but that is again not for this book.

In retrospect, showing up as my authentic self, being transparent and open, has allowed me to be me. In years gone by I presented myself as a superhuman (one of my team members described me as one) and almost untouchable. Now I know that this does not make people relate to me; I am not a robot. With this new-found awareness, it also now stops people responding to me with comments like 'it is alright for you' or 'for you it is easy'. Showing up as the real me has no doubt cost me some opportunities, but I now know that they would not have been the right ones for me. There is lots of learning to be had, and this process is ongoing. I am delighted to say that the opportunities keep presenting themselves. Most recently I was approached by an appointed co-chair of the UHLALA Group, RAHM Leadership Council, an organisation that supports young LGBTQIA leaders, or future leaders, to be provided with a community and programmes that will support their careers without boundaries.

TAKE CONTROL

- **Fear:** Now that I share my story so publicly, I engage in conversation. I spend time to understand other people's positions and opinions, allowing for sharing and debate. This in turn creates understanding and makes me human. I can continue to act from a position of strength and authenticity, showing others that they can achieve regardless of their 'difference'. Being a role model offers the younger generation an opportunity to identify, aspire and understand that everything is possible.

- **Trust:** A lot has been said about trust, so far; seeing the real me is all you need to get fully on board. Vulnerability is key to showing up. Brene Brown has opened this discussion right up.

- **Values:** They are possibly most poignantly described in this section. I have taken the initiative, when my life was completely falling apart, to seek help and through coaching and opening up, I have been able to rework the values that are relevant to the me of today!

RESOURCE PACK

By completing the personal chapter of this book, you have insight into my story and an opportunity to reflect on your experiences. Being able to share is a great opportunity to explore, in line with your needs. Check out the Fear, Trust and Values communities. You can find these in the social media links presented at the beginning of this book.

You can access the Resource Pack here:
www.annemiekehartmanjemmett.com

MY STORIES – WORK

FIRST IMPRESSIONS

CHALLENGE

You only get one chance to make a first impression.

MY STORY

Now this is quite a meaty subject. Much is written about first impressions and the value you should give to them. The takeaway from all the reading I have done is that you truly only get one chance to make a first impression. *Blink* by Malcom Gladwell is a very well-researched book on the subject, and I can highly recommend it.

I believe that first impressions are directly linked to people's fears and values. I cannot say that I have the research to back this up in detail, but I will set out the details I have gathered to support this statement.

As I have mentioned, trust and fear are intrinsically linked. In all the things we do, if we want to progress our relationships, in both private and business life, we should be aware that we are continuously– consciously or unconsciously– engaged in the process of creating trust. When we present ourselves, we can be sure that the person we meet is making an assessment of us, covertly or overtly. To explain this in the shortest way possible, they are trying to understand if everything aligns, makes sense. This happens all the time.

This question of alignment takes into consideration many elements, from the way you are dressed to the words you use, how you present yourself overall as well as how you communicate – do the words align with the goals and the overall presentation?

If this all matches up, we are ready to progress with confidence. In case this does not fully align, you may have to work harder. Working harder possibly means responding to more questions, explaining more, being more accommodating, until you arrive at the point of acceptance.

The point of acceptance can still mean that there may not be 100% trust, but there is sufficient for trust to outweigh fear. Joint values will help in 'bridging the gap'.

TAKE CONTROL

- **Fear:** Being aware of how people see each other and, more importantly, assess each other, will help with the reduction of fear. Here we are aiming to create an environment where we maximise openness. This is very difficult to achieve as we are 'conditioned' to think that people are hiding something – can we really take people at face value?
- **Trust:** When we are presented with people, we automatically make an assessment; when in our perception it all stacks up, makes sense, then we are able to trust.
- **Values:** If you share values, you are quickly able to 'shortcut' and trust, making first impressions work for you.

TEAMS FIT FOR RESULTS – THE RULER THEORY

CHALLENGE

Change is happening all the time.

MY STORY

I have worked with many teams throughout the years, and it is interesting to see what happens in the dynamic of long- and short-term engagements in the company. You have businesses keen to offer employment from cradle to grave – yes, even in this day and age. Note that it is their intention; however, they may not deliver on it. I was recruited not so long ago and, during this process, I actively requested to commit to a tenure until retirement; I know you cannot make this legal, but it is the sentiment that counts here. I duly did so, as this suited my situation (or so I thought). Somehow it did not work out that way.

I can also provide examples where employers are very keen to have short-term tenures to make sure that everybody stays 'fresh' and there is a lot of encouragement of creative thinking. This is fine if you agree it from the start – but it's not a sound approach for it just to unfold, to let people experience it, as it will create moments of fear, the 'when am I next?' syndrome. It directly undermines trust and likely the values you have set out as a business; of course, this is especially true if it is instigated covertly. If you all sign up to the methodology, you can create a vibrant and motivational environment offering skills, good vibes, an ever-changing environment and much more in return. There is nothing wrong with being transparent in promoting change, focusing on adding value. This allows teams to think for themselves and make healthy choices.

On balance, it is more likely that you will find yourself in the following situation. You may not have actively thought about this, in this way, but I find it a great methodology to explain what happened in my teams. I use this in every situation and have called it the 'ruler' (a straight strip or cylinder of plastic, wood, metal or other rigid material, typically marked at regular intervals, to draw straight lines or measure distances). We have all used a ruler during our school days.

WHERE ARE YOU ON THE 'RULER'?

Let's say you have got a ruler in front of you. It is 30 cm long and starts on the left with the number 0 and ends on the right with the number 30. Easy to envisage. When I start working with teams, I assess each person's capability as I see it, based on my experience and the role they will play in delivering the team's success. I plot each and every person on this ruler.

- 0–10: Beginners
- 10–20: Baseline
- 20–25: Potential stars or steady Eddies
- 25–30: Top performers

I trust you are with me on this so far. Now, my early plotting is an estimate based on years of experience. It is of course not an exact science, but it gives you a great head start on understanding how to plan your next steps.

What you will find in general is that the team you are working with will have members plotted all over the space on the ruler, although mostly they will be on the left side; as a guide, predominantly from 0 to 12.5–20. I hear you ask, 'Is this an issue?' Well, that will depend on the dynamics you expect from your team and how much you would like to maximise their results.

I once worked in a business that just wanted to 'tread water'. The team had learned, as determined by the leaders, to operate between 1 and 10: just keep things turning over, we have long-term plans with the business, we do not want to lose our high-profile customers, but we do not need to gain any either. Just keep it ticking over. You can imagine what happened when the private equity owners took over and were keen to maximise turnover and margins, and asked the same team to aggressively grow the business.

Back to the ruler. When I plot people on the ruler, I can do it in two ways. Number one: how are they performing today? Number two: how could they perform, if the business offered training, development and the right dynamics within the team– and how likely are they to engage? The saying 'you can lead a horse to water but you cannot make it drink' does apply here.

Additionally, in most teams I find that many operate between 0 and 20. Simply put, unless shown, they do not know what performance at level 30 on the ruler looks like. They are unconsciously not yet competent – they don't know what they don't know. Importantly, how do we get people from 20 to 30? It is very difficult to do this in the existing team. Unless you have had a superstar waiting in the wings, who has been able to 'lie low' for a period of time, there is only one solution: attract them from outside.

Now, attracting this performer with a level of 20–30 from outside is very difficult. Their job will be to move the performance of the others from below 20 to as close to 30 as possible. This means that this person will have to operate somewhere between 20 and 30 over a period of time. Slowly nudging the rest of the team upwards, they will need to perform below their normal pace or level to keep connection – many of you will find it difficult to engage in this build-up. For this reason, you need to identify your entry-level 30 performer on their attitude as much as their ability; there are not many of these people around.

I am sure you would agree with me that it is the business's responsibility to develop the people in the team, and even more so the people in my example – the ones told to keep the business ticking over. And I would wholeheartedly agree. It is the responsibility of the business to create the development framework for the individual team members to start to perform at the level the business requires them to. And remember, not everybody will need to perform at level 30. They may simply not have the ability to do so, and that is OK. The team will always be dynamic and have skills that you require at its foundation; as a leader, this is for you to understand in each and every new business situation. There are ways to maximise their results by putting processes in place that overcome this challenge.

The business is responsible for development, and I used to think in the past that if this did not have the fully desired effect, then I had failed as a leader. What I did forget in this situation is that I needed full buy-in and commitment from the team members. By talking openly about the 'ruler', its methodology and support structure, outlining the aims and overall strategy, I would immediately address people's fears. New management often means change, and the first question that comes up for each team member is, 'What does that mean for me?' Some primal defence mechanism kicks in – trust is a long way off at this stage, and fear can start to develop quickly and get out of control.

Be open about the assessment process you use, and engage with the team on the next steps, as this will reduce fear and create trust. By working together on joint values, you will start to create cohesion within the team and slowly together you will begin to move the team from performing averagely towards becoming top performers– with the right communication and by bringing in different expertise, using a catalyst and most importantly explaining what you are in the process of doing. Also remember that some people will just never be able to perform at that level 30. It is up to you to decide if this is OK; is it simply because they do not have the ability or 'bandwidth', or is it because they are obstructive? Now is also the time to understand how many people you need to perform at the different levels to achieve your goals.

Often, I hear leaders in these businesses say that people do not want to develop or come along, when really understanding why is going to change their behaviour.

It is because the leaders make a lot of assumptions and forget to communicate their vision and short- and long-term actions (think back to the playground – actively promote asking questions). Just because these leaders attend endless meetings and discuss the way forward each day does not mean that their teams are informed – assumptions here can really impact the success of the teams, or rather the lack of success. The teams need to be taken on the journey with the leaders. Offer an opportunity to engage (really engage, not just a 'town hall' meeting where they can listen to what has been developed). We attract individuals to our teams for the value we believe they will bring – but somehow when they are on board, we forget to check in with them to ask for their contribution. Or worse – we ignore them altogether. This is exactly what starts off fearful behaviour and an erosion of trust: not even taking impact on values into consideration. In brief, you do not stand a chance, either as a team member or as a business leader.

Now that we understand the dynamics, we can plot performance on the 'ruler'. Once you have assessed their development levels today and, with training, for the future, you can then also start to use the same methodology to check in with the team on a daily basis, asking how they see their performance each and every day. This does need to tie into your values and be signed off across the team and be highly valued – if not, it will work against what you are aiming to achieve.

Back to the new people you are bringing in. It is of critical importance that you start to bring in people from level 20–30 to achieve your objectives. It is up to you how you structure this in each different situation. It will depend on skills levels, behaviours, values and the overall 'bandwidth' of the individuals. However, you will be successful through its implementation.

To close, there is one thing that you will encounter while going through this process. The individual team members will also play an active part in this process. Some will relish this and will develop, sometimes beyond your expectations – this is great for them and for the delivery of your team's business objectives.

Do expect, however, that there will also be a number of people, over time, who come to a different conclusion – sometimes when you have spent a lot of money on their development. Their conclusion is that this business is no longer for them. Embrace their findings and support their next steps. If you try to keep them, sometimes only for their skill set, you will fail as a leader; and even if you manage to convince them to stay, if even for a short period, in the long run they will leave. Letting them go early is great for morale and you can see it as an opportunity to bring in new talent and fresh ideas.

For you, the leader, this also offers an opportunity. Consider the future performance of your team – does this require an adjustment? Re-plot the team on a new 'ruler' where you move the delivery expectation upwards. Move those who used to perform at level 20–30 to level 15–25, and then engage with new talent that levels the team up. As I set out from the beginning, this is not an exact science. You can play with this methodology to suit you and your style. Mould it, make it your own. Most importantly of all, in regard to reducing fears and improving trust, be open with your team about the process and link it in with your values. The results are yours for the taking.

TAKE CONTROL

- **Fear:** Being unsure of expectations in an ever-changing environment makes people fearful. Once the process is transparent and expectations are well communicated, the team members will feel that they can be the masters of their own destiny. In turn, this positively impacts team performance and allows all to act from a place of strength.

- **Trust:** Open communication creates trust. Knowing what to expect allows individuals to make the choices that are right for them.

- **Values:** Throughout this process, it is important that the employer takes the responsibility to develop and educate the team in line with the business expectations. Allowing this to take place will offer the individuals in the team the opportunity to make the choices that are right for them. This whole process allows you to be true to your values throughout and ensures that you retain a team keen to work together to deliver the results.

NO SURPRISES

CHALLENGE

Surprises are a good indication of failure in leaders.

MY STORY

Surprises are nice, right?! Since we were young, we have been told that surprises are great. You will receive something you had not expected, and the fact that somebody has been thoughtful and got you something unexpected is lovely. Well, in my business world, it does not quite work like that.

Why not? Well, in my world, events or situations that are not expected, good or bad, are surprises that we can well do without– in any business, whether private equity, privately owned, or listed on the stock exchange. Surprises are directly related to fear: the fear of not being able to deliver on your promises, which in turn directly undermines trust.

It is easy to understand that surprises linked to 'failure' are not that welcome. What I mean by that is that in a sales situation, last-minute underdelivered results are completely unwelcome surprises. The reason why is that products often need to have been made and put on stock to make sure that the production highs and lows are facilitated throughout the year. Also, commitments to banks may mean that you need to deliver revenue at the time it is expected and forecasted, not later than expected. Fear of failure will drive all the processes here. Leaders are keen to be assured throughout the business period that you are working, and they need to know the expected results so that they can start to manage their stakeholders. They need to provide other stakeholders in the business with the accurate (and sometimes disappointing) information that will allow these stakeholders to mitigate the impact of the expected results. This is so that all results can stay balanced throughout the year.

In turn, surprises that we would see as positive are also not welcome. Over-delivery of results may be great for the sales team because they are ahead of budget expectation – 'having things in the bag' is a great surprise! Looking at the broader business, though, this is an equally challenging problem to have. If as a business you are producing products, this surprise may mean you are short on materials. In turn, this may mean you cannot deliver on your promise within the agreed timeline, and a result like that could mean damage to the business. If you are a banker in this scenario, you will – if it happens frequently – start to become fearful; can you trust the predictions that the business is presenting to you?

I think you get the point that, in all situations, surprises are *not* good. In business, leaders are looking for predictability, as much as possible. This is exactly what businesses of today are focused on: excellent and accurate detail through customer relationship management (CRM) reporting. They do not really understand that customers and situations at customer businesses change. They think you should have somehow been able to predict even the situations that are now presented by the pandemic – really.

Where we should be realistic, however, is in understanding that, regardless of everything that has been highlighted above, change does happen, and not all events are predictable. Business leaders are looking for advance information from their sales teams, because they are the connector to the business representative or decision-maker; they must make sure to ask all the right questions to be able to present the detail maximising predictability. Knowing that you have a sales team in place that does all of this allows the teams to discuss strategy at the highest level, delivering the maximum results. This, unfortunately, hardly ever happens, as business leaders do not trust the sales team to collect this data accurately, which in itself tells you something meaningful: time to start sharing more information as a leader, introduce training where required, or restructure.

This then means that the leaders will question the sales team's input rather than its content, which in turn no longer focuses on the right outcomes – often severely impacting results and team morale.

In every role I have held in the past 25 years, I have been asked the following question: Can you let me know how many phone calls the sales team makes each day? This is so we can calculate their success rate. Clearly, activity has some impact on results, but it is simply wrong to think that activity only is a measure of sales success.

I will highlight an example here.

Salesperson number one focuses only on being on the phone and is making 50 calls each day for 20 days each month. This is a total calls level of 1,000. You would say that this is excellent sales activity. However, if the results of this call activity are 10 positive calls resulting in one sale, you would likely not be so impressed.

Salesperson number two splits their time between research and making calls, and they make far fewer calls for this reason; as few as 10 calls are made each day. Based on 20 days of calls, they only make 200 calls a month. On the face of it you would say that this is far less than salesperson number one– but due to the research and investment in understanding the businesses they are trying to sell to, number two has 100 positive calls, which result in 20 sales.

The learning in this short example is that I would employ salespeople with the profile of number two any day. Their call rate is 80% lower, but their success rate increases 2,000% with a net result level of 19 more sales.

Just take time to reflect on the above. This will change the results of your company once applied! For this reason alone, businesses and business owners should wake up to the fact that there is more to maximising results than just measuring activity in isolation. Measuring activity has its place, but *only* if you add other dynamics to this measurement.

Accurate predictability in numbers also takes away the surprise element. Key to all of the above is the ability for your teams to really understand the customer. How? You need to ask questions and make no unvalidated assumptions. You can make assumptions, but be sure to check these out with the person who makes the decision.

The more you are correct in your predictions, the more the leaders and stakeholders will start to 'leave you alone' to get on with delivering the business result. If you reflect on the above, it is no surprise that so much money is invested in data-driven systems that allow accurate pipeline predictions. These predictions are provided in great detail to ensure leaders are able to inform their stakeholders accurately, supporting success throughout.

One final comment. If, as a team, you get this right, all budgeting activities will be driven from the data provided by your systems. This means the days of 'pinning a number' on your budgets based on experience are over. Proper sales budgeting means that a planning action can then be organised, working across all functional teams.

TAKE CONTROL

- **Fear:** Down the line (think stakeholders here), there is also a responsibility to predict with accuracy. Impact can be significant for those informing finance houses. Missing result delivery against covenants is a serious breach of legal obligations.

- **Trust:** Open and clear communications throughout will allow prediction with accuracy. This allows the stakeholders to manage their interests, offering the opportunity to realign in good time and ensuring the delivery of results is in line with expectations.

- **Values:** This is quite a challenging part of the book. Many would see this as taking on a 'control freak' position. If you consider the detail of what has been expressed, you too will realise that the essence firmly sits in the values that you hold, not only in the company but also as a person.

RETAINING THE LIFESTYLE

CHALLENGE

Fear of loss drives all decision-makers.

MY STORY

Now that I have outlined fear and values in more detail, it is important that we start to look at how this is expressed. I vividly remember some work I completed in India. A very well-established and respected global e-learning company had asked me to come and complete sales training in their Delhi office. The fee I would be paid was INR1,000,000 – a fortune in India.

I fully admit that I am not your typical training provider, so why did they want me to deliver the work?

They were not looking for the typical training provider. They needed somebody who was able to impact the behaviours of the 'outbound call' team members. However, even more important was an in-depth understanding of the cultural differences between the call centre operators and the CEOs and global HR executives – the decision-makers – to whom they were selling high-value e-learning solutions.

I will not go into great depth about what the programme entailed. In India there is very little direct experience of western European lifestyles; this is difficult to convey as the typical outbound call team member is living with their family. Some don't even have access to running water but do manage to get to work each day in pristinely pressed white shirts! I have great respect for all of them.

So the question was how to tackle the insights here. It was all about painting the picture of the western European executive's life. It went a bit like this.

I told them that most people who are decision-makers in western Europe have a garden at the back of their house. In the garden you would typically find grass, and the regular rainfall makes weekly mowing of this grass a necessity, taking the United Kingdom as an example. With this simple piece of information, the whole team would be debating what this would look like – whether this was something most people would be presented with or if this was for the elite only.

We then progressed to discussing in detail the hobbies they may have. On purpose, I picked cycling as a hobby, which is very alien to India. With the European Cycle to Work scheme, many executives had opted to treat themselves to a new bike; many were using it to keep fit, join a cycle club or be active on the bike. This was a revelation to the team in India, and so far removed from their daily reality. In India, cycling means dicing with death every second.

What this did do was show the team members how they could research the 'typical' life of their decision-maker. When they called out to sell e-learning solutions, who would they get on the phone? What would be the drivers for their next actions? It was of critical importance that the team tapped into the decision-makers' fears, exploring the real reason why they were unable to sell their solution and how they should position themselves for success. Most times, decision-makers shy away from making decisions to bring in new providers because they perceive there to be risks!

If you are unable to address those risks head on, I can guarantee you that you will *not* be successful. The outbound call team had to understand clearly what the decision-maker would stand to lose if they made the wrong decision. Building trust quickly was critical. But the use of western European names for the people calling from India would immediately create distrust – exactly the thing you would want to avoid. Clearly their real name is unlikely to be Peter if you can hear they are calling from a centre based in India. Be authentic, right from the get-go.

In short, the decision-maker is at all times fearful of losing *everything* they have worked so hard to build: house, spouse, life. All the actions required from the outbound call team had to be structured in such a way that the decision-maker was protected, and throughout the call all objections were pre-handled prior to closing the deal. We all learned a lot from the four days that we worked together.

The success rate of the team increased by many multiples, and the INR1,000,000 was the best investment they ever made – their words, not mine. Being able to quickly tap into the essence of what the decision-maker feared most in making the decision, before then repositioning it to focus on the value it created, linked to the values of both the decision-maker and the company they served, was a total game changer.

Remember the decision-maker will do everything they can to protect their livelihood– this means both personal and work. Tap into this quickly by listening intently and creating trust – propose all and reap the rewards. And always, always deliver on your promise.

TAKE CONTROL

- **Fear:** By now you are starting to accept that everybody deals with fears, and these are unique to each and every one of us. Throughout the communications that take place, it is important to address how you protect the decision-maker by highlighting how they are secured. This means lots of preparation, leaving nothing to chance.
- **Trust:** Be authentic and well prepared.
- **Values:** In the overview presented above, you will see that there are many values that unite us, so be transparent and discuss them. The more you do, the more you start to see that you have a lot in common. This in turn creates trust and minimises fear.

IT IS NO SECRET

CHALLENGE

Trust your team to do the right thing and have your best interests at heart in everything they do.

MY STORY

Throughout the years I have been surprised by how businesses leave results to chance. In this day and age, delivering results is the key point of business. Now, we can argue about which results we want to deliver. For some, they are measured in USD, GBP or EUR; for others, they are more holistic and could mean a rating of five out of five for excellent service. As you can see, I am open to interpretation.

Let me start with an example. We have all experienced a road trip. Some of us go on an annual road trip, some a short shopping trip. To the other extreme, some of us travel around the world or participate in a type of organised rally from Paris to Dakar. When we prepare for these trips, we generally get a map out (well, at least we used to do so in the olden days; now we may plan this on Google Maps or any other digital mapping system).

My analogy often starts with the outline that we need to make our way to Rome. Key in this planning part is that we share with each other how we are going to get there. Sometimes it is important to discuss it in exact detail, as we are meeting along the way and there are tasks to be completed during the race. Maybe it is as simple as the fuel facilities along the route being few and far between so that anyone participating really needs to plan their way to make sure they do not run out. Also, we must remember to work to a budget and communicate that budget – no nasty surprises, remember! Whatever the reason, on road trips we plan the journey.

As part of all the above, we also make sure that we have the correct members in the team so we can keep moving. For instance, if you are going shopping for an item of clothing, it is most handy to bring the person with you who is looking to wear the item you are buying. If that is not possible, then we make sure we know all the details that are relevant, so we have a successful outcome.

If we are participating in a rally, we need to make sure we bring a navigator who can read a map with precision, and we may need to bring more experts who will make us more successful. In our private lives and at important events, the detail I describe above is a given; you are probably wondering 'what is the point of this overview?'

In work life, you will be amazed how often we forget, or are instructed *not* to implement, the basics. The number of teams I have worked with at peer level where I have been told that the goals should not be communicated is astounding. As recently as 2018(!) I have worked with team members at peer level who consider it totally unnecessary to discuss the end goal for the year. Worse, they *want to keep it a secret.*

Most of you will no doubt be laughing at this stage. I can see you now, saying that does not happen at your place! Granted, maybe the big-picture target is communicated in your business – well done. Comparing it to the earlier travel examples, you may have told your teams that you would like to end up in Rome. Great news! You have passed the first test. But now for further detail. Have you told them when you would like them to arrive by? How much money they can spend along the way? Would you like them to take the direct route or go another way? And yes, of course there is more, much more.

Why don't we bring this back to the workplace? You may have set out that you want to achieve a key goal, and this is often a monetary target. This is easy for a senior executive to set up. However, this often never happens; they forget to communicate with their teams, which would ensure they would receive it from the 'horse's mouth'.

Good businesses find a way to interrogate their systems to understand which targets are achievable, added to which there is a strategy designed to deliver on stretched targets, but I digress.

How many of you share some key indicators with your teams? What is the true cost price of your product? What margins do you want to make for the business to be viable? How much margin do you have to make for growth to be facilitated? And much, much more of this detail. The answer is often that 'Oh, we do not want to share this information. What if it is passed to the wrong person? What if the salesperson is sharing it with the customer? What if the salesperson is giving all of the margin away?' And there are more of these responses.

In my opinion, if you think any of these thoughts, change your teams! If you cannot trust them with the basics– or worse, if you feel challenged by these questions and you are unsure of your own capabilities, then *get out*! You have a duty of care not only to the business and its stakeholders, but also to the people in your teams. This is where fear, trust and values really hit the road. Are you prepared to make the right decisions as a leader for the longevity of the business? Or are you protecting team members because you do not want to jeopardise their livelihoods? Or worse still, are you protecting your own position in the business? Now that is confrontational! Do you ever ask yourself the question, come to a conclusion and *act* on it? Time for some self-reflection!

I have lived this scenario in each and every one of my jobs and roles. Some businesses have been inspirational, but they are in the minority. Most are secretive and ask their teams to put the tail on the donkey while blindfolded. It is really important for you leaders to figure out where you are on this journey, if only for the single reason to understand why your team fails to deliver each and every year. For those of you who do deliver, be honest with yourself – are you lucky or have you just planned it right?

There are many roads that lead to Rome. Communicate them and you have the best chance of being successful across the board.

TAKE CONTROL

- **Fear:** Don't hold back. Share what you know openly. It will allow others to see the full picture and support in delivering the desired outcome. Only then do we get individuals to be fully in and participating with all their knowledge. If you see that the other person is not holding back, participation is infectious.
- **Trust:** Sharing and being open delivers good engagement and participation. It allows each and every one of the team to be responsible for the end result, without holding back.
- **Values:** Here, in this example, it is so clear that sharing content, context and details is key for individuals and teams to work together. To be trusted to all move in the same direction, transparency and openness are key to inviting full engagement. They are the foundations.

AGILE TEAMS

CHALLENGE

Breaking the rules can benefit results.

MY STORY

This morning I had an interesting conversation in which we discussed the advantages of agile teams. I think it is of value to share some of the discussion here. The participants of the discussion were a retired USA-based lawyer and an English professional with a technical and engineering background. I had never worked with them; it was a chance meeting.

Agile teams are put in place to challenge convention. They are in general created to complete a short term project with the aim to work outside of any constraints. Large organisations that can afford the resources are often constrained by processes and staid methodology – too many 'rules' restrict progress.

The agile teams are created to deliver results quickly and without barriers. People who are brought together for these teams, from experience, generally have the following in common. From the outset they have all signed up to a joint methodology and specific outcome. They operate in a respectful manner to each other and work without any individual claim to success. They will claim success but only upon completion, where the team can claim joint success.

The people involved in very successful agile teams are prepared to look at skill sets across the team, they will pass work to the team members best suited to the task, and they do not hesitate to pull another member in halfway through completion of the task to get their view, input or help. There is total respect in the team for each other and, most importantly, there is a distinct absence of ego in these teams. Because the teams are created with a purpose, the individual members 'sign up' formally or informally to an 'operational code'.

Typically, these agile teams are very creative and can work to 'test and learn' principles. These individuals are there to 'own' the successes and failures. The business around them creates the space for them to fail frequently, learn and correct, and move forward at lightning pace. This is exactly what is promoted throughout.

It is relatively easy for the traditional part of the business to support agile teams in this first development phase. Enthusiasm and motivation are exactly what is pulling everybody forward, even in those areas of the traditional business that are involved in providing the agile team with the support they require to be successful.

Building the proposition in this early phase rolls on quickly.

The challenge for the team to remain agile will come if a business is putting expectations of revenue on it. Say a product is being developed, potentially already over a period of one or two years. The feedback from the market or the customers is so positive and the revenue potential so big that the established executives will internally discuss when to progress to potential revenue conversion. The likelihood that they will recommend to 'go early' is high.

The agile team will have created a specific dynamic and language or methodology over the period that they have been working together and, as highlighted earlier, they will work to a totally different process from the traditional businesses.

For the business to ensure it is able to deliver to expectation in the form of converted orders, undeniably it will want to add additional resources to the agile team, making sure that the business is able to deliver on its promise.

The agile team will recognise that they need this support and will welcome the additional resources and skill sets. However, with this addition also comes the greatest danger to the success of the project.

For the agile team to be engaged and effective, the introduced members should take great care in bringing the team along, integrating them into the traditional business in a considered way. I have seen very few good examples of this in my professional career.

Too often, the added members are of a different make-up, a different type. They are much more focused on short-term delivery times and profit and loss – correctly so, in my opinion – yet lack the sensitivity to bring the agile team on board with what is required for the long term. This can be done with care, and quickly, if the added team members are sensitive to the dynamics that have been established so far. They must remember that the team has had to be successful in getting this far! They have done a great job to date.

Get off track at this point, and the whole project will be in danger, if the new team members are also the new leadership, not sensitive to the group dynamics and solely focused on slavishly delivering results to the senior executive. Be warned that they will achieve one thing, extremely quickly: disengagement! I have seen this in practice, and it is astonishing to see how quickly this happens. In a matter of days, the team that were previously so in tune can even stop operating entirely; they start to sit on their hands. Fear will quickly consume the team members. Test and learn is often stopped, and finding fault (at worst, being exposed by the leader) is prominently active. The team will stop in their tracks. They will wait for instructions, not be engaged, and ownership will reduce only to those jobs they are allocated to complete. There will be no anticipation across the project, and the leader will realise, often when it is too late, that they are on their own. This then often results in more authoritarian behaviour, which in turn results in even less engagement from the team. I have witnessed that this can be fully accomplished within a six- to eight-week timespan, with disastrous results for the mid to long term.

This becomes even worse if the incoming team members, who are likely a different 'breed', start to criticise the working methodology to date (not surprisingly, this was different, as they had a different brief). They might muscle their way in and claim all successes as their own. I could list many examples here, but naming and shaming does not add any value. The challenge is highlighted. Be aware simply so you don't walk into the same trap.

Now that we are aware of what happens, it is simple to prevent it. But how?

The agile team is keen to be accountable, every step of the way. They have had autonomy throughout the project, so it would be odd if new members came in who did not respect this. The agile team members in turn understand that the long-term success of the product or service depends on creating the infrastructure required to deliver long-term success. All it takes is for the incoming additional resource to listen to the agile team's struggles, experiences and successes; to engage and communicate how they can best support and help, taking away those mundane tasks that the agile team is unlikely to excel at. In fact, the agile team often cannot wait to hand them over, in any case. It would, as you saw above, be a mistake to ignore them in this process. Sharing success across the team is fair and offers opportunity to all. The skill set is different, and one would not have achieved the joint success without the other, so celebrate it! And most of all, respect what each and every one brings. This may be very different, but we know diversity brings challenges and, with respectful behaviour, a greatly improved outcome.

Agile teams can fast-track organisations beyond all imagination. Respect each other and respect what each skill set brings to the overall success. Creating an environment without fear, promoting trust based on the values you jointly set out, can deliver results beyond your imagination.

TAKE CONTROL

- **Fear:** Open communication across the teams is key to joint success. Regular goal-driven meetings inviting broad participation and good listening skills will fully aid the effectiveness of the team. Everyone needs to truly understand that each and every person has a role to play. Understanding what has gone before is also key to overall success. Respect each and every employee and the expertise they bring to the team. Value them, and engagement and participation to deliver the result will be maximised.

- **Trust:** Critical here is that you value each person for what they bring to the team. Actively inviting participation is key to starting to understand each perspective. Work on the understanding that all involved are looking for success; nobody is there to boycott. It is the leader's responsibility to keep the project on track and maximise the team's expertise and input, challenging them in what they are able to deliver. Give the people autonomy within a framework to deliver results beyond expectation.

- **Values:** Businesses are increasingly working in a matrix type setting. This means we need to start to show behaviours that are more and more in line with the business values, while offering specific technical expertise in our chosen field. When we are able to reduce fear through excellent communication skills (sending and receiving), we will be able to build trust through respecting what each and every person adds to the team, living our values throughout.

BOX CULTURE

CHALLENGE

Skills are not frequently recognised as being transferrable into other industries.

MY STORY

Building on the introduction of agile teams, let's explore the benefits of what I call 'box culture'. Let me explain so we can set off from the same point together.

Businesses are rightfully keen to employ team members who are able to add value from day one. This can take place in many ways. Either you have a specific skill set that is very particular to an industry and have delivered success in that industry with this skill set over and over again, or you have a particular attitude that neatly fits with the business, and the employer may see an opportunity to explore– or, more likely, exploit– that attitude. And quickly.

I am sure we can all sympathise with the following, but I will keep it close to home so I can speak from experience. Throughout my career I have worked for many different organisations, from (most recently) manufacturing and engineering through to fast-moving consumer goods. Throughout these years I have come to understand that many businesses deal with the same challenges. Commercial growth processes are, at their core, equal. Of course, there are specific elements to any business or industry – I am not challenging the different approaches businesses take here.

If we adhere to the 80/20 rule, 80% of business growth can be secured for each business in a similar process-driven way– especially if the professional you hire has been involved in many different businesses and industries and is competent in process analysis and implementation while understanding buyer behaviours and drivers. They have the advantage of diversity; they have seen different things work (or not work) in different businesses; they are agile and can pivot to suit the business challenge in front of them. Most of the time they are quicker in picking up what is required, they are good at decision-making and they will take the team forward with autonomy and ownership of the challenge ahead.

You will recognise those times when you express and present extensive and diverse experience across cultures, countries, industries and businesses – only to be told that they have had applicants for the role who more closely match the experience required. Why are individuals who are able to present a diverse work experience often not rewarded for this ability? Why do employers like to 'play it safe' when adding new members to their team? This is because only now are organisations ready to recruit to the values that flow out of their business.

Still, as a priority, businesses are keen to find 'like for like' experience. Where possible, they would like you to show that you have done it all before in the same industry – and preferably in a business very similar to the one you are looking to join. After all, the business is looking for predictability. They will be rewarding you with a salary (compensation for your input of time), but they are there to receive a predictable, almost certain, return on their investment. That is their real reason. Are they right or wrong? Well, I suppose, on balance, they are neither right nor wrong. This is just the way in which they can create predictability in the very uncertain process of recruiting and appointing.

Can it be done differently? Absolutely, it can be done differently.

How should we look at this? Let's explore another option together. If a business is confident about the fact that their purpose and supporting values are the overriding factor why people want to join their team, they could consider recruiting according to these main held beliefs and joint values. This means they will combine experience, skill set, attitude and values during their evaluation process. They are, critically, focused on selecting team members in line with business 'fit'. These businesses look for a different kind of predictability. I would argue that these businesses have taken the approach that they can teach the incoming team members the specifics of their business or industry with a defined and well-prepared and developed on-boarding programme. What they have decided is that they cannot teach the cultural elements, like attitude and values, quickly enough (if ever) and that these are the ones that count towards progressive business success.

I would welcome businesses to be more open-minded about the opportunities that they are leaving on the table by their preference for quick predictability of the creation of success. Here, in my experience, they may deliver the $, € or other currency results – but at what cost? And we should specify that the 'cost' includes not only the factual costs of recruitment, retention, laptops, phones and so on, but most importantly, the cost of lost opportunity. Opportunity is lost simply because a predictable route is selected rather than a more engaging route that may require input and development in those early days.

TAKE CONTROL

- **Fear:** Many businesses are very happy with the box model, simply because it has been repeatedly proven to work and deliver results. No challenge here. Those of you who are already applying this approach, or are in the process of doing so, be brave: you are and will be rewarded. However, it does contain an element of risk.

- **Trust:** Challenge yourself here, as per the outline: what would happen if you could trust the process more? You would increase engagement and, at the same time, tap into the opportunity presented to you.

- **Values:** Here you find that behaviour-based searches in line with the purpose will offer the best returns across the board. Retention is enhanced and all team members can align to the joint purpose, delivering maximum results.

HANDSHAKE VALUES

CHALLENGE

There is a different value in old values.

MY STORY

Here you need to make sure that you are not 'tripping over yourself', or at least that is what I find to be a challenge from time to time. Recently, I was told that relying on a 'handshake commitment' is what old people do – apparently it is seen as old-fashioned.

I decided to explore this a little more. Are handshakes old values only, or is there still a place for them in today's world? Handshake commitments are unwritten commitments between two people. Most of the time they exist based on trust and are an expression of honour. If you 'shake on it', this means it is formally confirmed that you will execute the thing you have agreed on. Pride, honour, trust and values are at play here. It is certainly what I was taught when I was young, and I hold it in high regard. And for me it is alive and kicking.

How is it for younger adults? In exploring this over days, weeks and even months, I can report back on the following. Younger adults agree that a handshake is a commitment you make, yet they would make a significant adjustment. The younger adults would add that, after they make this commitment, situations and/or conditions may change that would in their view warrant the 'handshake deliverables' to be withdrawn.

I find this an interesting insight. Being aware of this addition may therefore make you ask for additional commitments: set a timeline to the handshake or, in short, create more clarity around what you are jointly signing up to. This is so there will be no misunderstanding between the two parties, no misalignment of expectations.

I find here that open questions – trying to really and genuinely understand the other person's motives, drivers and commitment without judgement – bring us all much closer together. There is no ill intent, just a difference in understanding what we are committing to at any moment in time.

To recap here, there is still value in a handshake, but a bit more focus on the conditions of commitment will stand us all in good stead.

TAKE CONTROL

- **Fear:** Be clear on what you are committing to, and over what time frame, and communicate how changes in indirect events may change the handshake commitment you have made.
- **Trust:** It all starts here with communication, so be clear and outline what you do accept. Do not rely on assumptions. It will enhance trust if you are detailed and do include time in your agreements.
- **Values:** It is such a good example, and it is clear that handshakes are still part of today's values mix. The 'sell by date' is shorter than it used to be, but this may very well have something to do with the fast-paced environments and continuous change that we are experiencing through the introduction of new technology and 24/7 open communication channels.

IT'S ALL ABOUT THE MONEY

CHALLENGE

Money is the result of good business, but some of us think it is the purpose of good business.

MY STORY

This more or less refers back to the real question: why are you in business? If the answer to this question is 'for the money', then keep reading, because you are missing a trick. I cannot highlight often enough that, yes, all businesses are in business to (at worst) break even, in the long term, and (at best) to exceed their own expectations on revenue or margin. Ultimately, this is in cash. More money.

For some, this is the only reason why they get up in the morning and 'do their thing'. It may be that they focus on the money simply because it allows them to do something else that offers engagement, joy and 'nourishment of the soul'. Good for you.

If the focus is on maximising the output/outcomes, you may want to look a bit more broadly at the engagement. The business is solving a problem in society; that is the purpose of the business. The group of people who are focused on purpose delivery are going to be most successful if they find commonality in their values; that is, they share something so fundamental to their being that they behave totally in line with each other. The people you attract are participating in keeping these values at the forefront of their day. These values guide them in everything they do; they are successful because of these values and the behaviour they display. Fear is apparent from time to time, and it can be discussed in the safe space, with values the overriding guide; each day, individuals and the team subliminally build trust. That is a sound base from which to operate.

Your response to this may be 'I see no pitfall here yet', and you would be totally right. There is not one here, simply because you have a homogeneous group, operating as one, keeping each other on track. When someone – small groups or the leader – goes off track, the group learns that they need to get back on track. Yes, it really is that simple, with only one condition for success: you need to have signed up to this way of realignment from the outset. Again, it is not difficult – but it is a prerequisite.

So, this section is called the 'values pitfall'. Many organisations take shortcuts, sometimes justifiably so. I can imagine that when you are growing at pace, fulfilment seems a higher priority than recruiting and developing team members in line with the business values, let alone sourcing people 'outside of the box' as this requires investment of time and money, one or both of which you may not have in abundance.

However, you could instead be a 'big' business hiring to feed the machine and stay in line with shareholder expectations. We have seen a lot of examples here during and following the pandemic. Survival is at the forefront of everybody's mind, and it is in the interest of all involved, right? Plus, you often hear 'we have our values right, so what is the issue?'

Exactly– that is where the values pitfall is! We think we have them, yet upon examining them more closely, they are like one of those really nice, colourful sticky plasters. You have seen those sticky plasters – blue or pink, there to attract attention, or the ones with comics on. If you attach one of those sticky plasters after a scuff, they immediately make you feel better.

It doesn't work any differently with values! You have them, they sound great and to the outside world they even look spectacular. The leadership often is able to express great sentiment by leading with these values. But have you tried scratching beneath the surface? No? Well, let me do this for you a little – again, from experience.

I can refer back to experiences where the leadership is incredibly authoritarian and so out of tune with the workforce – they are fully unaware that they have made this happen, by the way. They would also express that they actively request participation but highlight that the teams just don't participate– but they never ask themselves why. The response would be that the team has disconnected for fear of being made to look foolish.

The leadership quote all their values with conviction in the local and national press, as well as on their own communications. They forget to stop and check in with their teams to make sure they are aligned. Here they need to *really* listen. This is a very dangerous place to be as a leader, and as a business, as your teams actively disengage. This is often manifested as key members leaving, significant 'water cooler activity' and different groups forming in the team.

I have worked in a business where the team started to mock the executive for their external upbeat, values-driven messages. The executive was totally oblivious to the internal conversation. On the outside it looked great, but it was not reflected on the inside. At worst, new starters came and joined due to the external 'ra-ra' – a total misalignment and therefore a waste of resources. Keeping the business on track became a real challenge and everything but authentic. And believe me, in the end, everybody notices.

The details outlined above actively create fear and break down trust– and it can be even worse than that if the values are then changed or adjusted without involvement of the wider teams. Be careful in the process and its engagement. It is not complicated to get this back on track, but it does take time. Think and plan to maximise your impact. Leaders 'just' need to be aware, open up and start the process of value development and alignment all over again. Be genuine and ask actively for participation – be non-judgemental and open to different views.

Your business success will depend on it!

TAKE CONTROL

- **Fear:** If the only measurement you operate in your business is money, you may be adding to the insecurity of your teams. In most businesses I have worked in, the money is never enough– not quick enough, not high enough etc. Consider adding purpose to your reason for being. Not just as a sticky plaster but as the real reason for being in business.
- **Trust:** Being able to be clear on purpose, values which will define the level of money required, is a healthy way of creating commitment. Trust will flow from that.
- **Values:** Participation from all team members in defining the values will create a committed team, able to maximise the results; this will include finan cial results as an outcome – not a reason for being.

RESOURCE PACK

You have completed the 'work' section. The most effective way to start to maximise your success is to move from a one-dimensional to a three-dimensional way of communicating.

ONE-DIMENSIONAL COMMUNICATION

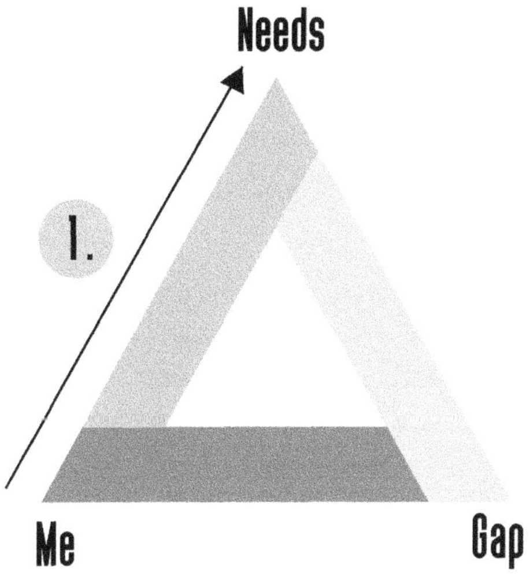

1. *There is a direct line between 'sender and receiver'; lots of room for error, through assumptions.*

THREE-DIMENSIONAL COMMUNICATION

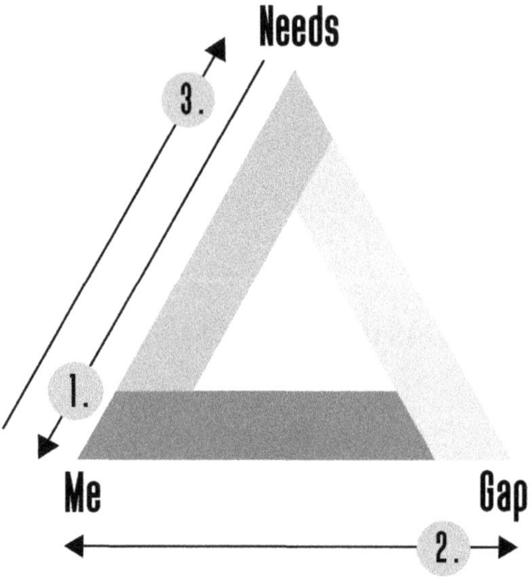

1. *Understand the need of the person you are communicating with – let them talk.*

2. *Understand where the gaps are that others may fill– maybe not as well as you or your company does, but they are in the same space.*

3. *Present your offer or perspective in line with the need that you have understood and the gaps you have identified. This will maximise your opportunity each and every time.*

YOUR FUTURE IS TODAY

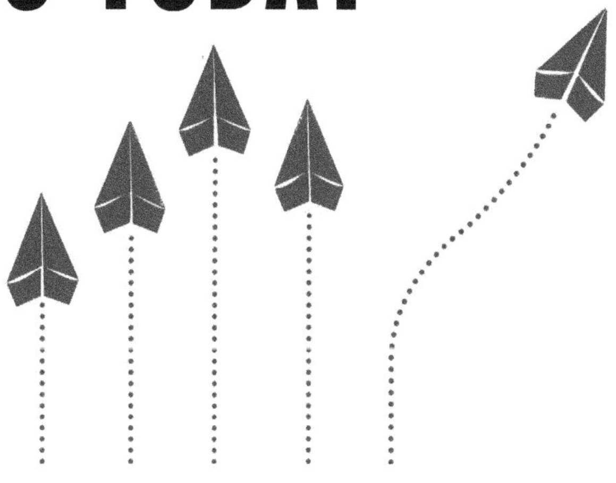

PIVOT

SELF-GUIDANCE

Get out there – make a noise.

MY STORY

I took myself off to write this book in a new environment. I did that for a number of reasons, but the main reason was to have some new inputs and, with that, some creativity. I did not just squirrel myself away to a house in the middle of nowhere; I decided to go abroad and live a semi-different life, still by the beach, but in the sunshine rather than a harsh Covid-ridden winter. I was also keen to see some different things after two years with minimum travel, speaking to people with a different point of view, life experiences and social economics.

During my last assignment, I was confronted with a whole new business vocabulary. The words that stood out were for us to 'test and learn' and most importantly to 'pivot'. I am not sure if this is an American term or now used in global business. I have sat with it for a while today while watching the ocean swell and the surfers 'doing their thing' along a perfect stretch of beach.

At the same time, I was trying to find the answer to a question that one of the other pool users– we lane-swim for a while each morning– asked me a few days ago: why write the book now?

As I was seeing these surfers go out, one starting off to catch the wave sooner than the other, I saw them lying in wait for the perfect wave to bring them exhilaration and a chance to hone their craft. That was followed by more waiting, more looking and listening to the sounds and conditions around you. I came to the realisation that this was why the 'book now' moment had arrived.

For years I have been working in businesses of all sorts, in many different countries, and for years I have been consumed by the notion that we can go faster and be bigger and better as teams, as businesses and as individuals.

Last year, I took a different approach. I started to take ownership of my personal and business life. Not purely in a planned way: life just did its thing and threw me quite a few curveballs. The easy route would have been to respond in the way that I have always done, but that would have provided me with the same results as I have always had.

I stopped and asked myself the question: what do I want? I worked with some amazing coaches during this period and started some outline planning on what my life would look like going forward, how it could be future-proof.

I have always been convinced that we should live life to the full – that this is no rehearsal, so we should enjoy, live and be kind.

That is often easier to say than to put into practice, so what did I do? I did a pivot. 'Pivot' does not mean 'change everything completely', but in the dictionary the word is described as follows:

'The central point, pin, or shaft on which a mechanism turns or oscillates.'

And just like the surfers in relation to that wave, I had waited for years to position the links between fear, trust and values. I knew at a very early stage that values were key to the mechanics of a business, but the way they were communicated often completely missed the point, not mentioning the way they came about or how they were used to reduce fear and create trust.

As the future is today, now is the time for me to ride that wave and share the stories and my insight with the aim of providing some tangible ways for the reader to explore, grow and create for themselves.

For me, staying engaged is super important, so I have decided that I need more than one input. Yesterday's quote from Leadership First on LinkedIn outlined it well: 'You often feel tired not because you've done too much, but you've done too little of what sparks a light in you.'

My 'pivot' has resulted in a successful interim assignment where I have been able to add real value and deliver aggressive growth results in a short time frame (with none of the barriers that you could find in a permanent role), a book that I will complete in the set timeline (set by me) ready for publishing and a strategy for presenting my photographs on a website, supported by some exposition events.

Will it all be successful? Yes, I have no doubt; success is much more than volume of sales or award recognition. Having started and finished the book is a result all on its own. Outside recognition is nice and a 'cherry on the cake', but that is not why I set out to share my thoughts, experiences and findings.

Many people are confronted with fears in life and in the workplace. Allowing people to own these and working together to overcome them, with this book offering a different viewpoint, is all I set out to do. Awareness is power and the catalyst to do things differently.

My 'pivot' has resulted in an updated set of values that I live by every day. These are now my guiding light. It puts me in full control: I engage in those things that I believe in and I own my life, which means there is no place for fear. This in turn maximises trust in myself, my surroundings and in the businesses that I work with.

FIND YOUR TRIBE

SELF-GUIDANCE

Life is about making choices, always.

MY STORY

Now this is a very interesting section. Over the years I have thought about how 'finding your tribe' is relevant. Let me start by explaining what I mean by finding your tribe.

As for what a tribe is, the eminent Seth Godin defines a tribe as 'a group of people connected to one another, connected to a leader, and connected to an idea. For millions of years, human beings have been part of one tribe or another. A group needs only two things to be a tribe: a shared interest and a way to communicate.'[1]

If you are interested to know more, by all means read up on all there is to know and form your own opinion. I can identify with the outline they present and would like to outline how this is relevant to me and my values, which then directly addresses 'fear'.

---

1 Seth Godin, *Tribes: We Need You to Lead Us* (2008).

Years ago, possibly when I set out to build my career, it was all about progress and making a life for myself. I worked for large, generally American, organisations that offered me the opportunity to grow. They invested in my development and, through this development, I could attain the goals I had set for myself. Even though I was not interested in the title, the money or the status, I was keen to be able to provide for myself, so climbing the ladder became necessary. I did very well for years within this setting.

However, the industry I had chosen to work in was not really a long-term option for me. Unless I wanted to be a hotel owner or hotel manager, which was not my aim, I knew I had to get out.

The next few years seemed to be more about earning money than developing myself. I managed to do very well for myself and started to work in sales roles, ultimately working with teams as their sales lead in various contexts, including as sales director, director of business development, chief commercial officer and interim sales lead. I earned huge bonuses and was very well off overall.

However, this quickly started to really bore me. If I had stayed, then I would have achieved financial independence more quickly, but I wanted to achieve more and more diverse results.

After working with a number of coaches throughout my career, I am now free to make more balanced decisions on what comes next. I can make life more diverse and interesting with extensive varied inputs. It has offered me the opportunity to stop, write a book and put my corporate life on hold for a short period.

Following the writing of this book, I know I will continue to add value, because I am really good at delivering commercial results with teams. I will do so being an even more rounded individual. More experiences will result in more authenticity and more value, both for the company and for me as a person.

Being able to choose my tribe– like-minded people and companies– I am able to maximise my input, and the results are beyond what I could have imagined all those years ago. I feel calm and fulfilled. No doubt you can write books about finding your tribe, but that is not my mission. However, highlighting this has been important in my life.

DON'T DREAM, PLAN

SELF-GUIDANCE

Put lots of things out there and let it come back to reward you; stop striving! Take time to reflect and practise some self-care. It does not have to be hard all the time.

MY STORY

Often when I speak to people, they tell me that they have a dream. They tell me all about the dream and how it will change their life. For years I used to listen and respectfully nod and, at some point, we would go on to discuss something else. In one extreme case, after being told about the same dream for years, I challenged the dreamer about why he had not done it yet; we lost touch shortly after.

Over the last few years, I have been coaching some young adults, and often the dream is a part of the early conversation. They tell me all about their dream. Now I ask them one question:

What is it that prevents you making that dream a reality?

That question stops everybody in their tracks. Dreaming is nice – it offers an unrealistic sense of security. However, as you can see in this book, when you plan, you achieve.

The summary for this section (and yes, it is kept short on purpose): start with a dream but ensure you quickly convert it into a planned reality. That is, if it is really important to you!

SCHOOL OF LIFE – PHD

SELF-GUIDANCE

Look at how many of your old colleagues come back into your life to ask for reflection and guidance. The School of Life offers value to all.

MY STORY

I was talking to an acquaintance a few weeks ago. This was in the USA, the location where I had decided to travel to and rent a house to write my book. We talked a lot about changes in legislation and life in general after the Covid pandemic. I had chosen to stay in San Diego, La Jolla in particular, and here they had just changed the law on permitted development. We were discussing the virtues of progress in general and the development of towns and accommodation in particular.

We then progressed the conversation into how to be heard. And his view on being heard was all about education. His belief was that you can only have a platform from which to speak and be heard if you have educated yourself beyond most of your peers. He has advised his children to get educated to PhD level as, in his view, that is the only way for them to be heard in the future and have the ability to change things going forward.

Of course, I understand his argument, and have a lot of understanding for his position, but my belief is that there is also a place for people to be heard without the validation of a university-issued PhD. If you have lived and have a story to tell, this can also be of great value to others if you are prepared to listen and guide, rather than tell.

In my view the School of Life also issues a 'Having Lived It' PhD that is well worth obtaining. This does mean that you need to 'live' and experience many different events, be exposed to many cultures, show extensive amounts of interest. You need to be involved in many different things, 'lose your shirt – almost' and have the blisters on your a** to show you have been on a bumpy ride. But most of all, you need to have the ability to listen. This PhD of life can prepare you well for being heard. It is how you use the information you have collected to date in combination with the requirements to 'fight the good fight' that can set you apart and keep you engaged.

In reflecting on this chapter, to select one over the other would do both an injustice; the best preparation for success in life is education *and* life experience. Some are still on the journey, while others have completed this early and are reaping the maximum rewards.

OWN IT!

SELF-GUIDANCE

Be transparent and kind, own your mistakes and successes as it will motivate others, and you can share a life lived.

MY STORY

In reading all of the pages so far, you have found out that it is all about experiences in life! That is what makes me me and you you. Cherish your uniqueness and hold your own life against the light. Do your values override your fear at all times? Or are you impacted by fear more often than you would like or even care to admit?

I decided a number of years ago that living with fear (of losing my job, my livelihood, my relationships) was not a brilliant investment of my time or a good use of my brain power. I think we all worry too much and too often, without really thinking it through.

My moment of epiphany came when I stood to lose it all. This had been building, even while I was making great business decisions and delivering some brilliant results. I hadn't realised that to build a consumer brand with your own funds is a near impossible task, if you have two other business initiatives running full steam. I was financially so overstretched, loving the 'hype and high' it gave me, that I distinctly remember needing to be in London for a business meeting and being able to just about scrape the cash together to buy the train ticket.

On another occasion, I was offered some paid work which required me to travel to Nigeria. Fortunately, the client who joined me paid for the meals and all costs during the trip. Quite frankly, on those occasions when I was left to fend for myself, I used the fruit bowl in the gym to cover a snack gap.

I distinctly remember the time when I was invited to rejoin a business. At the time, I really needed any income and had to brave it out during the conversation – they expressed they could not really afford me. I told them they could indeed not afford me, but I was able to 'do a deal' so that they could. I held my ground, was offered the job and a six-figure salary with significant bonuses, and was back in the saddle. The value the company received was multiples of the renumeration they paid me. A win, win, win for us all.

From the stories above, you can see that it has not always been easy. But working hard and being creative and smart has kept me moving forward, delivering the successes I enjoy today.

I have never shared my financial position with anybody, but thought it important to share it here, because adversity delivers great clarity. It also starts to make you think about what is really key to you. There are two critical points that have contributed to a change in my life:

1. During this period, I came to think about what would happen if I really lost everything. After a lot of soul-searching, I came to the conclusion that it would unburden me, and I would have the skills, network and enthusiasm to build my life up again. Ever since I came to that realisation, I have never looked back.

2. To prepare for my future, I have sought out some personal coaching, and this has revolutionised my life! Everything I do now is from a point of values, and this keeps fear at bay while generating trust.

Implementing the above has offered me opportunities that previously I did not believe possible.

My advice is: own it! And be kind to others, and everything will flow to you.

ON BALANCE AND IN SUMMARY

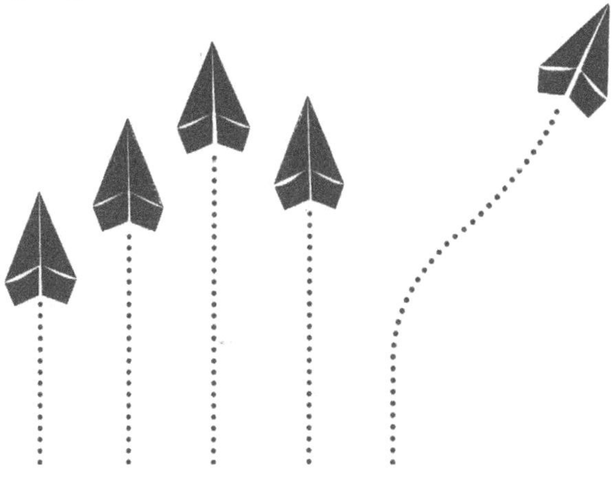

You have completed the journey! In reading my story and by implementing the 'take control' conclusions, you are ready to further explore the opportunities available to you, each and every day. Congratulations on making the change!

Being aware of what is really happening 'behind the scenes' will get you to look closer and design a way forward that allows you to take control and fits with both your personal goals and the organisational goals.

You can now:

- Use **fear** to keep you safe while letting debilitating fear go.
- Build **trust** to create more rewarding relationships.
- Live to the **values** that matter to you.

You are ready to choose to live your best life and find your tribes.

FEAR

In my review, I have come to the conclusion that fear is a good thing as long as it is used to keep you from harm. As soon as it starts to take on any other dynamic, like influencing your decision-making to retain what you have built up, then you should review, address and adjust.

Fear that is out of control – do check in with yourself here – is actually messing up both the person and the business they operate in. Remember: fear is a choice.

TRUST

The cornerstone of everything. Yes, it really is that. Unless you are able to create trust among the individuals who operate within the team, you are nowhere. Trust is at the core of success. A team with members who trust each other is able to deliver results beyond imagination. They work together in tandem and without ego. They pass the 'to-dos' around the team, finding the best person to do the job, fitting in with their skill set. When done successfully, it starts to become effortless and increases motivation without boundaries. This is possible; I have named many examples. When there is no trust (and it only takes one person to mess things up), you will find quite the opposite: teams will sit and wait for instruction, and they will not share and work together to achieve a common goal. Unfortunately, the latter is much more prevalent than the former.

Many team members have told me through the years that the secret of their success is the fact that decision-makers 'like them'. I have always argued that this is not the case – I still agree that this is not the case – however, in writing this down now, I realise it allows them to convert the opportunity into new business. It is the fact that they trust their contact to look after them and 'do the right thing'. Ultimately, in their communications, they express implicitly or explicitly that they commit to deliver on their promise. (We should not mistake this for 'good salesmanship' or 'professional sales behaviour' – it takes much, much more.)

VALUES

A lot has been said and written about values. Any self-respecting business will set out, hopefully with team engagement, the values that support its business purpose. Too often, unfortunately, the values are a 'label'– they look and sound good, often following trends in tune with social developments. This is often a great way to attract the best in the business and an excellent recruitment strategy. However, unless the values are lived throughout the organisation, the engagement is short-lived and may only last 18 months. From my experience, you, the new member, will start out living the values and drive them across the organisation, only to find out that they are shallow. Working hard in a senior position to get change effected will ensure some progress. But even the most dedicated new team member will, over time, get disengaged if they feel they are the 'Joan of Arc' in the business. Your senior team needs to be fully on board, and their behaviours *must* be in line with the purpose and agreed values. If not, remember the example of the executive who could only name four of the five values they designed, completely confirming that they did not live them each and every day. That is when you are on shaky ground in ensuring your teams can operate without fear and in complete trust.

IMPLEMENTATION

What does it take to align all of these in a headline, and for this to stay very manageable? You have now gained access to a toolkit to take control.

BEHAVIOUR

Yes, this is really where it starts! I can beat about the bush – but this would be selling you short. We need to have everyone signed up to a set of behaviours, creating an environment where there is no space for fear and full trust is paramount. This means your recruitment process needs to select on values and behaviours. But just selecting to these criteria is not enough. You must work to them each and every day. Most importantly, the team members must hold each other to account. If they have signed up to these values and behaviours from the outset, then you have contracted with them to keep you all aligned. It is not only your duty to do this, it is everyone's duty to do so. Try this on for size: your team will also hold you to account as the lead, should you stray. Now that is a game changer!

PURPOSE

Firstly, know your business purpose. Really do the work here – don't just apply the label that you feel will make you look great. Really put in the work that sets out the reason for being, how you are solving real issues.

FIND THE 'BEST OF THE BEST' TO JOIN YOUR TEAM

How often do we convince ourselves that we just cannot afford those people who will make the difference to our business? In some cases, of course, that is correct. So how about being more creative and hiring people with the correct attitude? They should have the experience you require, but they do not have to be the 'prima donna' – a homogeneous team will work on supporting each other, reducing fear, building trust and operating according to the shared values. Remember, you can train them, and there are many ways to reward individuals and teams; no longer is money the only reward system that drives success.

Be creative and work outside the 'traditional model'. Millennials expect you to do so. They will be looking to be offered a mix of financial rewards, 'good initiatives' in which they can get involved, flexible times and locations in which to work, and company-wide bonus schemes which can take many different forms; for example, signing up to sustainable businesses like Patagonia, where credits are offered at a higher multiple than cash, or simply offering cash bonuses to reward team performance.

(Note: from my experience, team rewards *only* work if the whole team is challenged to deliver each and every day – you need an excellent performance management system with *everybody* buying in. Experience has shown me this is not easy, but it can be done.)

Don't just assume that you cannot afford to attract great people to your business; engage and discuss. Find a solution that rewards both of you.

SET OUT THE BUSINESS GOALS

Work together across the business to define your business goals. Make them challenging; use data you have collected throughout the year(s) to support the objectives. Get the teams involved, and commit each and every one of them to the goals. Listen, adjust, pivot during your development process. Once your goals are set, stick to them. Get them signed off by each person individually and by the team in total. Now is the time to contract.

PERFORMANCE MANAGEMENT SYSTEM

All of the above is great and perfect scene-setting. You contract with each other from the outset. You agree between you what each is willing to contribute and which framework 'rules' you are agreeing to work to, and then you are set.

But, as we all know, life takes over and we drift from the best intentions we set at the start. Therefore, although it is not nice to consider, it is required that we also agree how we can get each other back on track. This is best agreed from the outset, when we are all motivated and engaged without any ambiguity. If the time comes that you need to realign, then you can both do so, following the agreement you set out from the start. You will notice that I have outlined that you *both* need to participate, because it is only when a framework is developed cooperatively that it will have the value you both believe will offer the best results. I will leave it to you to see which system best suits your organisation, but I can imagine regular check-ins will keep you on track; one-to-one conversations and quarterly, half-yearly and annual reviews are a standard way of making this work. Of course, you can create something that works for you all, but the key here is to do these check-ins regularly. If you leave it too late, you start to misalign and could easily come off track. Getting back on track takes time and will mean that you miss out on opportunities.

HOPE

So that is all clear and makes sense, and of course we are all doing this already.

Are you sure? Maybe you want to think again; there is always room for improvement, right? Maybe you are– great!– although you are still unfortunately in the minority. Maybe you are doing some of it; if so, well done – you will be rewarded. In case you are trying to get things started and have the best of intentions, excellent – keep going, you will get there. If this is an eye opener, fabulous – my investment of time and sharing my experience has so been worth it.

In all cases, get in touch; the feedback from you all will make an excellent follow-up from which we can all learn and explore, making things better for all of us.

Now that you have completed your journey and started to take control of your life, share this book with others who will benefit from understanding how to use fear to take control, while not letting fear debilitate them. It will allow them to maximise the building of trust while getting clarity on their values and finding a way for their tribes to live their best life.

'Annemieke supported me through a restructure of the business, and her advice was fundamental to its success. Her guidance resonated clearly during an uncertain time. The coaching we received on business development created immediate results within the team. I highly recommend.'

ALIX WATERHOUSE, FOUNDER & CEO OF MY METHOD – 2022

'Annemieke is one of those people who seems to make a success of everything she turns her hand to (I bet she was in every sports team at school!). Many people display great capability in strategy or developing teams. Annemieke possesses the rare capability of strengths in both. She recognises key market opportunities and can translate them to strategy. She also has an eye for talent and can turn that potential into performance.

'Annemieke is a thought leader (and author) around trust and company culture and has developed expertise in digital marketing technology. It has been a pleasure working with Annemieke on numerous growth projects over the past seven years.'

SIMON GOODISON, FOUNDER & CEO OF SMARTER NOT HARDER

'It has been a great experience to have Annemieke join me on our start-up journey for a unique and "category-creating" product. Her knowledge and experience goes without saying, so I wanted to point out two attributes I find admirable and a differentiator. Firstly, she clearly is a leader and commands respect, but she works up and down the team, building chemistry at all levels and is a motivator through her own actions. Secondly, she is not only a strategic thinker, but she is a "doer". She dives into the details and will work alongside her colleagues to get things done. I find both of these qualities refreshing in a modern leader.'

TOM WOOD, PROJECT DIRECTOR

'I can honestly say that you are a very special person! I haven't met anyone like you. You are incredibly smart (like very smart), funny, have so much wonderful experience, and you are very perceptive. I too will miss working alongside you on a daily basis. Having you on the other end of the video call always makes me smile.'

RUSSELL ZIEGLER,
BUSINESS STRATEGIST

'I wanted to send a note along to you personally to say just how much I appreciate and enjoy working with you. It has been an absolute pleasure to get to know you, work with you on this team, and learn from you. You have a way of listening insightfully, acting purposefully, and bringing people together thoughtfully to achieve results. It has been inspiring to get to know you and I regret that, in that same vein, we really only scratched the surface. Please keep in touch!'

HELEN DIODORE, GROWTH HACKER

'Annemieke is an inspiring leader with a clear vision on which path one needs to follow to be successful. As a leader she is giving her teams a very structured way of working, not only to obtain the overall supervision of the different processes within a company, but more importantly, to be able to give more freedom and responsibility to each individual team member. I remember Annemieke as a strong leader, but what I respected the most was the fact that she made it very clear that being successful means having a good work/personal life balance. "Work smarter, not harder".'

**DAVID VERHAEGHE,
SENIOR BUSINESS CREATOR**

'It has been a pleasure working with Annemieke. I got to know her as a dedicated, creative, to-the-point leader. Annemieke has been a great mentor to me, especially during our many sales business travels; she knows how to get the best out of you and taught me to always think 10 steps ahead. She is a great asset to any team; strategic and result driven. Annemieke moves an individual, the team and the business forward!'

LINDSAY LASSOOY,
SENIOR BUSINESS CREATOR

'Annemieke is highly ethical, highly meticulous and works well at director level. Someone who has many ideas of her own but also a professional who knows how to deliver others' ideas. In sum, she is strong both strategically and operationally – a rare blend and a true safe pair of hands.'

CHRIS MIDDLETON, FREELANCE STRATEGIST & AUTHOR OF *YOU CAN BE AS YOUNG AS YOU THINK*

'Some of the words that come to mind when thinking about Annemieke are business savvy, marketing guru, relationship builder and mentor. Annemieke knows how to get the best out of you, knows how to push to get results but at the same time gives you the support needed to deliver to the best of your ability.

'I not only thoroughly enjoyed working with her but also learned a lot about areas I had previously no experience in, for which I cannot thank her enough. A true leader.'

ANDREW STARK,
CO-FOUNDER & SENIOR PARTNER

CONGRATULATIONS!

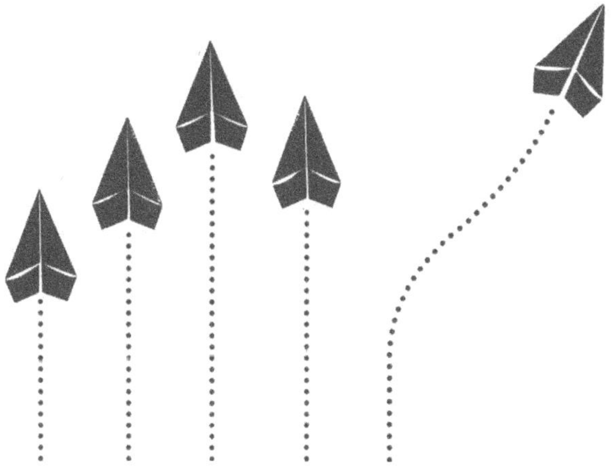

You have worked through all of the details – well done! In the process, you will have become more aware of your values and learned how to build trust and manage your fears more effectively. You are fully in control of living your best life. As promised at the start of this book, you will have progressed. Now is the time to work through the initial assessment, as the final action in completion of this book.

FINAL ASSESSMENT

I have the ability to change behaviour in others.	Agree/Unsure/ Disagree
I lack control.	Agree/Unsure/ Disagree
I dislike work.	Agree/Unsure/ Disagree
I lack the skills to do my job.	Agree/Unsure/ Disagree
I don't see the big picture.	Agree/Unsure/ Disagree
I am not really able to engage.	Agree/Unsure/ Disagree
I maximise my productivity whenever I can.	Agree/Unsure/ Disagree
Tasks I have to do seem to take a lot of effort.	Agree/Unsure/ Disagree
I believe challenging conversations are a form of conflict.	Agree/Unsure/ Disagree
I am stuck.	Agree/Unsure/ Disagree

This is not the end!

Now download the resource pack and continue to take control:

- Download a copy of your workbook, including the assessment you went through at the start, and upon completion of the book; this offers you control and tracks your results.
- Book a FREE 20-minute call with me to chat through your journey; I am interested to learn more.
- Try the Fear, Trust and Values Community. This is a community of people who are proactive in managing fear, choose to behave according to their values and build trust; sharing allows us to grow.
- Find the explanation of the three-dimensional communication diagram.
- Gain access to other multimedia sources, including videos and articles.
- Find the opportunity for collaborations in the future.

You can access the Resource Pack here:

www.annemiekehartmanjemmett.com

SHARE YOUR FEARS

Now that you have worked your way through the full book, you may be keen to share your experiences or alternatively learn from others. For this reason, we have set up a 'share your fears on a postcard' facility.

Write your anonymous (secret) fear on the big blank side. Be as creative as you want to be. It is my intention to collect them and then post them on Instagram and ultimately get a postcard book printed with the best submissions.

On the reverse you will find the address to send the card to. All it takes is a stamp.

FEAR

IS A CHOICE

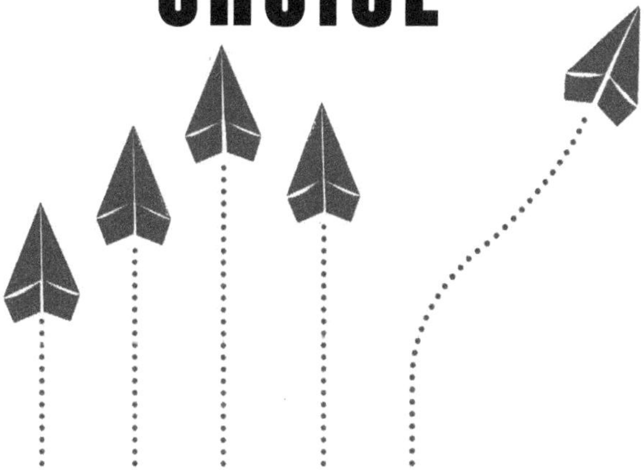

TRUST

BRINGS US TOGETHER

VALUES

OWN THEM

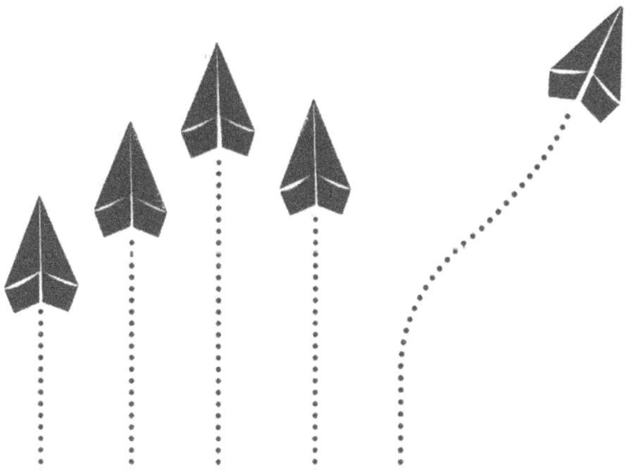

Lightning Source UK Ltd.
Milton Keynes UK
UKHW041434051022
409919UK00008B/4